THE UNOFFICIAL

THE "I LOVE MY NUTRI BULLET" RECIPE BOOK

200 HEALTHY SMOOTHIES for Weight Loss, Detox, Energy Boosts, and More

Britt Brandon, CFNS, CPT

AVON, MASSACHUSETTS

Published by
Adams Media, a division of F+W Media, Inc.
57 Littlefield Street, Avon, MA 02322. U.S.A.
www.adamsmedia.com

ISBN 10: 1-4405-9208-X
ISBN 13: 978-1-4405-9208-9
eISBN 10: 1-4405-9209-8
eISBN 13: 978-1-4405-9209-6

Printed in the United States of America.

10 9 8 7 6 5 4 3 2

Library of Congress Cataloging-in-Publication Data

Brandon, Britt.
The "I Love My NutriBullet" Recipe Book / Britt Brandon, CFNS, CPT.
pages cm
Includes index.
ISBN 978-1-4405-9208-9 (pb) -- ISBN 1-4405-9208-X (pb) -- ISBN 978-1-4405-9209-6 (ebook) -- ISBN 1-4405-9209-8 (ebook)
1. Smoothies (Beverages) 2. Health. I. Title.
TX817.S636B73 2015
641.8'75--dc23

2015019028

The information in this book should not be used for diagnosing or treating any health problem. Not all diet and exercise plans suit everyone. You should always consult a trained medical professional before starting a diet, taking any form of medication, or embarking on any fitness or weight-training program. The author and publisher disclaim any liability arising directly or indirectly from the use of this book.

Always follow safety and commonsense cooking protocol while using kitchen utensils, operating ovens and stoves, and handling uncooked food. If children are assisting in the preparation of any recipe, they should always be supervised by an adult.

Many of the designations used by manufacturers and sellers to distinguish their products are claimed as trademarks. Where those designations appear in this book and F+W Media, Inc. was aware of a trademark claim, the designations have been printed with initial capital letters.

This book is unofficial and unauthorized. It is not authorized, approved, licensed, or endorsed by NutriBullet, LLC. NutriBullet is a registered trademark of Homeland Housewares, LLC.

Cover design by Sylvia McArdle.
Cover images © iStockphoto.com/carlosgaw; kaspri/123RF.

ACKNOWLEDGMENTS

I would like to thank everyone who has inspired me, educated me, and supported me through the journey to achieving greater health. My husband, Jimmy, and our children, Lilly, Lonni, and JD, have always been my inspiration to achieve better health, and I am so blessed to have the opportunity to share my lifetime with a wonderful family whom I adore more than I ever dreamed possible!

My editors at Adams Media have given me the amazing opportunities to create and develop intriguing titles, helping to make a dream-career become a dream come true. I feel very lucky to work with such an outstanding team of people.

Rosa Samoa with the International Sports Sciences Association (ISSA) has always been an outstanding resource for nutrition and physical fitness education. Creating and providing courses and material that have been profoundly educational, she and ISSA have made it possible for health-minded people like me to pursue higher education in a field that evolves and improves every single day.

Finally, I would like to say "thank you" to everyone who has helped me integrate healthy living, quality nutrition, cooking and smoothie-making techniques, and alternative medicine information into my (and my family's) life. It has been such a fun and exciting journey to this healthy new lifestyle, and I want to thank all of my readers and blog-followers of UltimateFitMom.com for sharing in the love of learning about all things nutrition, health, and wellness to improve the quality of life for us all!

CONTENTS

INTRODUCTION

It's not quite a blender and it's not quite a juicer. Instead, the NutriBullet is a device that combines the best features of both to offer you a path to healthy living. Using it, you can create smoothies that contain both juice and fiber (unlike those created by most juicers, which tend to remove the fiber). The equipment is simple to maintain (cleaning takes around a minute), and it's relatively inexpensive. And you can make up bags of vegetables and fruits beforehand in pre-measured amounts. All you have to do is pull them out of the fridge, put them in the NutriBullet, and *voilà*! A healthy, wholesome smoothie.

Kick-starting a healthy lifestyle that revolves around powerful, supportive healthy foods may sound challenging. Those imagined obstacles can stem from a lack of knowledge about healthy foods, few ideas for healthy snacks and meals, or a dislike for "healthy" foods that is further compounded by cravings for unhealthy alternatives. Luckily, using the NutriBullet and this book will help anyone adopt a healthy diet easily and deliciously. The NutriBullet's innovative extractor blades release the nutrients from within every cell of the superfoods combined in these recipes, unleashing powerful, potent nutritional benefits into every last sip of these super smoothies. By liquefying the superfoods, the NutriBullet makes their fiber, vitamins, minerals, antioxidants, oils, and enzymes bioavailable for ultimate absorption into the bloodstream and utilization throughout the body. Countless delicious combinations of superfoods can be stacked into a NutriBullet and blended into smoothies for healthy meals or snacks. The NutriBullet not only makes a healthy diet tasty, exciting, and visually pleasing, but also makes healthy meal- and snack-planning simple.

You can consume one of these smoothies in a fraction of the time that it would take to eat and drink all of the individual foods it contains. The NutriBullet is one of the best investments you can make for your health, no matter how much time or culinary experience you have.

Whether your goal is to get healthy, stay healthy, or improve a specific area of your health, the results you seek are well within reach. In the quest to achieve optimal health, the easiest and most effective lifestyle changes focus on diet and exercise. Moving your body has countless benefits and is a major part of any health-focus regimen, but diet is an aspect of daily life that can transform your health. After all, the vitamins, minerals, antioxidants, amino acids, phytonutrients, fiber, and protein that your body needs in order to function are found in the foods you eat.

Consider the benefits of consuming a clean diet: By eliminating toxins, the excessive sugars, sodium, and preservatives in processed foods, and the unhealthy fats in the foods that litter the daily Standard American Diet (appropriately termed "SAD"), the body can use clean superfoods as high-performance fuel for every aspect of its functioning. It can more easily deal with health issues such as obesity and chronic fatigue as well as avoiding, minimizing, or eliminating diabetes, cancer, and other conditions that have been shown to be directly related to diet. When you feed your body natural foods that are packed with essential nutrition, you will not merely function—you will thrive. With superfoods in your NutriBullet cup every day, all of your body's systems work together to become an effective energy-boosting, hormone-maintaining, overall-health-promoting network that helps make every day healthier than the last.

With this book of 201 delicious recipes, you can quickly find the perfect smoothies for your tastes, needs, and goals, and begin enjoying all of the benefits of better health today!

Note about Juices

Throughout this book a number of the smoothies use juices, especially apple juice. Here's a recipe for homemade apple juice that you can use instead of the store-bought stuff. Packed with fiber, vitamins A, C, and E, minerals such as calcium and magnesium, and unique antioxidants like quercetin, this quick and easy supercharged NutriBullet version of apple juice contains no chemicals, preservatives, or harmful additions.

18 OUNCES

Fuji apples, cored

2 tablespoons aloe vera juice

¼ teaspoon ground organic cinnamon (optional)

1½ cups purified water

1. In the 18-ounce NutriBullet container, combine all ingredients.
2. Blend until all ingredients are thoroughly liquefied and combined, 30–60 seconds.
3. Store the juice in the NutriBullet container with the included airtight lid in the refrigerator. Consume within 24–36 hours to ensure maximum nutrition.

While many recipes have called for fruit skin to be removed, the NutriBullet smoothies use the skin as well as the pulp. The NutriBullet's patented extractor blade technology is able to liquefy the skins of apples, pears, figs, and cucumbers efficiently, blending them seamlessly into your favorite smoothies. As well, nutrition contained within the skins of these superfoods is more potent than that within these fruits' flesh. Core your fruits, but leave the skins on for an extra burst of nutrition.

CHAPTER 1

SUPERFOODS: SUPER FOR YOU AND YOUR NUTRIBULLET

A WORD ON NUTRITION

Carbohydrates, proteins, fats, vitamins, and minerals are the macronutrients and micronutrients that provide your body with the fuel and energy it needs in order to function. Antioxidants and phytonutrients support and protect the functioning of the body's intricate systems. These macro-, micro-, and phytonutrients can all be found in the fresh fruits, vegetables, nuts, and seeds that compose a healthy diet focused on clean, whole foods. The cells within these foods that store the major nutrients a body needs to thrive are encapsulated and protected by a cell membrane. NutriBullet's extractor blades release those nutrients and its exclusive cyclonic action liquefies the ingredients, providing easily absorbable nourishment to the digestive system, bloodstream, and entire body. Every sip contains fiber, vitamins, minerals, and phytochemicals that would otherwise pass through the body, losing much of the nutrition content.

When you consume superfoods rich in nutrients, you unharness the power of nature to develop benefits that can be seen everywhere from your skin and eyes to your teeth and hair, and felt everywhere from your muscles and digestive system to your energy levels and clear mental functioning. Specialized phytochemicals unique to certain fruits and vegetables can provide protection against illness and disease. You can tailor nutrition to your needs by selecting specific blends of fruits, vegetables, and additions. The superfoods that are combined to create these delicious "NutriBlast" smoothies will not only add delightful shades of color to any diet, but contribute to the new vibrancy experienced by the smoothie sipper.

Apples

Apples come in a variety of hues thanks to their rich polyphenol content that acts to protect cells, improve immunity, and combat inflammation. Polyphenols also act as powerful antioxidants that contribute to optimal functioning and health of the cardiovascular and respiratory systems. The fiber content in an apple contributes to proper digestion, helps regulate blood sugar, improves cholesterol levels, and helps maintain a feeling of fullness after eating.

Avocado

Creamy and delicious, avocados are a great-tasting addition to super smoothies. With dozens of varieties to choose from, the light-tasting avocados that pack pantothenic acid, copper, vitamin K, and B vitamins also provide lycopene, beta-carotene, and carotenoids while adding healthy fat to your daily diet. Improving metabolic functioning, cognitive processing, and cell protection, avocados are well worth adding to any super smoothie.

Bananas

The potassium-rich fruit that decorates the counters of millions is not only sweet and delicious, but packed with essential nutrients that promote healthy heart functioning and improved digestion, and can enhance athletic endurance. As a low-glycemic food with rich stores of essential vitamins and minerals, bananas provide the perfect low-calorie addition to any super smoothie.

Beets

Beets come in two hues, red and gold, as determined by which betalain pigment gives them their color. Whether colored by betacyanin, which provides the red variety with their red-violet coloring, or betaxanthin, which creates the yellow of the gold variety, the antioxidant and anti-inflammatory benefits of the betalain remain the same. Add to these phytochemicals' antioxidant power the detoxifying and metabolism-boosting benefits that help maintain overall healthy functioning of the body's systems, and you've got a sweet treat in beets that improve the taste, color, and healthfulness of any super smoothie.

Berries

Packed with vitamin C, manganese, fiber, and phytochemicals, berries are a wonderful addition to any smoothie. They supply powerful antioxidants that promote immunity and prevent dangerous cellular changes, have anti-inflammatory properties that alleviate arthritis and chronic disease, and contribute anthocyanins (the natural phytochemicals that give berries their vibrant coloring) that provide health benefits to the bloodstream, the eyes, the skin, and much more!

- Strawberries
- Blueberries
- Raspberries
- Blackberries
- Acai berries

Carrots

Packed with bright beta-carotene, carrots add sweetness and splendid nutrients to any super smoothie. With vitamins A, and C, that do double duty as powerful antioxidants, added to the phytochemicals such as their carotenoids and polyacetylenes, carrots are a delicious addition to any super smoothie recipe.

Citrus and Pineapple

Citrus fruits, with their sweet and tangy flavors that tantalize the taste buds, take any super smoothie to a new flavorful sensation of taste sensation and healthfulness. Adding these fruits to your daily diet provides you with ample amounts of the B vitamins, vitamins A and C, and minerals such as copper, pantothenic acid, and potassium. Further, these fruits protect your health and boost your immune system with healthy doses of fiber and by acting as powerful anti-inflammatory antioxidants.

- Oranges
- Lemons

- Limes
- Grapefruit
- Pineapple

Coconut Oil

One of the lesser-known oils is one of the most beneficial . . . and can be added to any super smoothie. Coconut oil not only provides a bounty of vitamins and minerals, but also contains medium-chain fatty acids that can transform your health by improving every aspect of your body's functioning.

Garlic

Belonging to the allium family, to which the onion also belongs, this powerhouse of a smoothie ingredient can take a savory smoothie to new levels. Improving the antioxidant and anti-inflammatory benefits that all super smoothies provide, garlic helps to soothe digestive dysfunction, improve metabolic functions, and enable better breathing and mental processing.

Ginger

This spicy and sweet addition is more than just a flavor-enhancer. Providing vitamins A, B, C, and E, a host of minerals, amino acids, and unique enzymes, a single slice of ginger can add a variety of health-boosting benefits to any super smoothie. Helping the heart, brain, digestive system, respiratory system, and even mood, ginger can add sweet spice to your favorite flavorful super smoothies!

Grapes

Small and mighty, the gorgeous grapes that come in a variety of colors and flavors can up the ante of your super smoothie with a combination of nutrients that help with anti-aging, respiratory health, blood sugar levels, and gastrointestinal functioning. With their healthy doses of vitamins and minerals that also provide the body and brain with antioxidants to protect the cells and improve functioning, grapes are a tasty addition to your favorite super smoothie.

Kale

Packed with more than 1,000 percent of the daily recommended value for vitamin K, one serving of kale provides immense nutritional benefits that support and protect all of your body's functions. Adding a deep green vibrancy to any super smoothie, the simple addition of one or two leaves is all a NutriBullet user needs to improve the vitamin and antioxidant content of a favorite super smoothie.

Kiwi

The kiwi can add a delightful tropical twist to any super smoothie. With its impressive provisions of vitamins and minerals, this superfruit adds protective antioxidants that promote cell health and defend against harmful oxidative processes that can wreak havoc on DNA. Credited with clearing respiratory issues and improving immunity against microbes, bacteria, and viruses, this sweet little green fruit is worth adding to any super smoothie.

Mangoes

Once called the "fruit of the angels" by Christopher Columbus, the mango not only offers powerful health-promoting and protective nutrients but adds intense flavor to any super smoothie. With a beautiful color that shows off its rich stores of beta-carotene, carotenoids, and flavonoids, this delectable fruit makes for a sweet ingredient that adds great taste and better benefits with every serving.

Melons and Cucumbers

These hydrating fruits come in a variety of colors and add succulent sweetness and plentiful nutrition with every ounce. They're packed with essential vitamins, minerals, and phytochemicals that combine to improve health while protecting the cells from harm.

- Cantaloupe
- Honeydew
- Watermelon
- Cucumber

Nuts

With rich stores of vitamins, minerals, and phytochemicals, the most astounding benefits of nuts are packed in their provisions of omegas. Omega-3s, omega-6s, and omega-9s combine to boost brain health while improving the taste of your super smoothie. With anti-inflammatory and antioxidant compounds that also protect the body against dangerous cell changes, nuts are an invaluable and tasty addition to any super smoothie.

- Almonds
- Walnuts
- Cashews

Onions

The spiciness of onions can add a zip along with health-promoting power to any super smoothie. Providing an abundant array of vitamins, minerals, and phytochemicals that promote healthy functioning of the body's processes, onions also bring unique enzymes, antioxidants, and anti-inflammatory properties to the table.

Papaya

The papaya provides papain, a phytochemical similar to pineapple's bromelain, helping to fight oxidative damage to the cells, improve blood flow, and maintain proper enzymatic activity throughout the body. With its sweet, delicious flavor, this fruit packs a healthy provision of vitamins, minerals, and phytonutrients.

Peaches and Nectarines

The bright yellow of a ripe peach or nectarine signifies its riches of beta-carotene, a powerful antioxidant that supports the immune system's functioning while protecting cells from oxidative damage. Along with the powerful antioxidant support, peaches and nectarines protect eye health, heart health, and brain health with their provisions of B vitamins, choline, and potassium.

Pears

The fiber-rich pears that sweeten any smoothie also provide vitamin C, which helps in the body's process of regenerating vitamin E; both vitamins fight free-radical damage and improve immune system functioning. The copper in pears further supports the fight against cell damage, helping to maintain healthy skin and system functioning, and their fiber keeps the digestive system clean and clear.

Pomegranate

The pomegranate not only supports the immune system and protects against illness and disease but maintains optimal cholesterol levels of the blood and supports the brain and nerve communication. Through the vitamins, minerals, and amino acids contributed by the pomegranate's tasty jewels, this fruit is able to improve health and protect against serious illnesses and disease; one study has even shown the remarkable ability of pomegranate to prevent and/or reverse the incidence of prostate cancer.

Seaweed

With calcium, phosphorus, and magnesium, seaweed can help improve and maintain a number of areas of health. Through the building of bones' density, the maintenance of muscle health and strength, and the support of energy, endurance, and stamina, this all-natural protein source that also provides essential vitamins and minerals is a smart, simple addition that can transform any smoothie into a super smoothie!

Seeds

Seeds are another simple super smoothie component that are frequently overlooked. These tasty morsels can improve the health of the entire body while maximizing the functioning of the brain. With powerful antioxidants, rich stores of vitamins and minerals, and a combination of phytochemicals that protect the cells, support the synthesis and processing of nutrients, and improve metabolic functioning, simple seed additions can boost benefits by the teaspoonful!

- Chia
- Flax Seed
- Hempseed

Spinach

Spinach is a deep-green, light-tasting vegetable that adds an abundance of vitamins, minerals, antioxidants, and unique phytochemicals to any super smoothie. Protecting the body from cancerous cell changes, spinach's glycoglycerolipids add to its rich content of vitamin K, calcium, and vitamin C, helping to improve immunity, boost cognitive functioning, and maintain the health of the entire body.

Spirulina

Regarded as one of the most bioavailable sources of protein, the powdered algae spirulina has become a popular nutrient-dense addition to any smoothie for a boost in vitamins (especially A, C, E, and K), minerals (phosphorus, magnesium, and iron), antioxidants, phytochemicals, and amino acids.

Sweet Potatoes

A rich source of vitamins, minerals, and powerful phytochemicals, the sweet potato adds a creamy texture, sweet flavor, and delightful orange hue to any super smoothie. Easy to blend using the NutriBullet's patented cyclonic technology, a sweet potato can be added to any super smoothie of your choosing, improving its taste and health benefits.

Tomatoes

Tomatoes are a beautiful and bright smoothie ingredient that, while light-tasting, can load your super smoothie with nutrients that improve the health of your entire body and brain. They help to maintain eye health, improve cardiovascular functioning, fight obesity, and regulate cholesterol in the blood.

CHAPTER 2

13 SMOOTHIES FOR BETTER IMMUNITY

With super smoothie recipes that combine ingredients designed to improve your health with great taste in every sip, the NutriBullet can help you improve your immunity and fend off illness. Citrus fruits, vibrant greens, apples, melons, celery, cherries, ginger, and garlic are just a few of the players featured in these immunity-boosting super smoothies. Sweet or savory, the flavors that combine to create these delicious any-time-of-day smoothies will help you create a smoothie you want that helps you achieve the healthiness you deserve.

Powerful vitamins and minerals combine with phytochemicals to combat illness and disease. At the same time, they protect the body's systems and cells from harmful changes that can result from oxidative stress, toxins, or prolonged inflammation. The super smoothies in this section boast fruits, vegetables, and additions that not only taste great when blended together, but boost immune system functioning to optimize health and minimize illnesses (mild, moderate, or severe!).

DARK DEFENDER

vegan, green, sweet

In this recipe, dark berries combine with bright red cherries and vibrant spinach for a phytochemical-packed smoothie that provides vitamins A, C, and E, and phytochemicals that pack a punch against cell oxidation and inflammation. The NutriBullet liquefies and combines these berries, cherries, and spinach perfectly with the antioxidant-rich green tea for a potent immunity-boosting blend of bright deliciousness.

18 OUNCES

¼ cup blueberries, frozen
¼ cup blackberries, frozen
¼ cup cherries, pitted
¼ cup spinach leaves
1 cup green tea, cooled

1. In the 18-ounce NutriBullet cup, combine all ingredients.
2. Blend until all ingredients are thoroughly liquefied and combined, 30–60 seconds.
3. Consume immediately, or store with an airtight lid in the refrigerator for no more than 3–4 hours.

PER SERVING

CALORIES: 63	FAT: 0 G	PROTEIN: 1 G
SODIUM: 7 MG	FIBER: 4 G	
CARBOHYDRATES: 15 G		SUGAR: 10 G

IMMUNITY BOOSTER

vegan, green, sweet

With antioxidant-packed ingredients that provide bountiful nutrients to safeguard health and prevent disease, this super smoothie can perk up your day while warding off colds, flus, and chronic disease. Tasty enough to sip at any time of the day, this vitamin-, mineral-, and phytochemical-packed smoothie will protect you from illness.

18 OUNCES

½ cup spinach

½ large Granny Smith apple, cored

½ large orange, peeled

½ medium grapefruit, red or pink

1 cup purified water, divided

1. In the 18-ounce NutriBullet cup, combine the spinach, apple, orange, grapefruit, and ½ cup of the water.
2. Blend until all ingredients are thoroughly liquefied and combined, 30–60 seconds.
3. Add remaining ½ cup of water, as needed, to achieve desired consistency.
4. Consume immediately, or store with an airtight lid in the refrigerator for no more than 3–4 hours.

PER SERVING

CALORIES: 87	FAT: 0 G	PROTEIN: 2 G
SODIUM: 12 MG	FIBER: 4 G	
CARBOHYDRATES: 22 G		SUGAR: 18 G

FLU FIGHTER

vegan, green, savory

This savory blend of antioxidant-rich ingredients makes for a spicy snack or meal that not only puts pep in your step but provides all of your body's systems with essential support to fight the flu. You get a filling serving of veggies, with the added benefits of vitamins A, C, E, and K, to help protect you against the flu during flu season and against other viruses year-round.

18 OUNCES

¼ cup spinach
½ teaspoon seaweed
½ tomato
1 clove garlic
1 tablespoon red onion
1 cup green tea, cooled

1. In the 18-ounce NutriBullet cup, combine all ingredients.
2. Blend until all ingredients are thoroughly liquefied and combined, 30–60 seconds.
3. Consume immediately, or store with an airtight lid in the refrigerator for no more than 3–4 hours.

PER SERVING

CALORIES: 22	FAT: 0 G	PROTEIN: 1 G
SODIUM: 12 MG	FIBER: 1 G	
CARBOHYDRATES: 5 G		SUGAR: 2 G

SORE THROAT SOOTHER

sweet, paleo

A sore throat can have numerous causes that range from bacteria and viruses to a hearty evening of boisterous laughter. Providing your throat with a soothing combination of honey, cinnamon, and almond milk along with powerful anti-inflammatory, antioxidant support can help prevent the development of irritation or illness. This delicious mix of powerful antimicrobial, antibacterial, antiviral ingredients not only soothes a sore throat, but revitalizes the entire body.

18 OUNCES

1 cup cherries, pitted
½ teaspoon ground organic cinnamon
½" piece ginger, peeled
½ tablespoon apple cider vinegar
1 cup vanilla almond milk
1 teaspoon all-natural honey

1. In the 18-ounce NutriBullet cup, combine all ingredients.
2. Blend until all ingredients are thoroughly liquefied and combined, 30–60 seconds.
3. Consume immediately, or store with an airtight lid in the refrigerator for no more than 3–4 hours.

PER SERVING

CALORIES: 331	FAT: 3 G	PROTEIN: 14 G
SODIUM: 162 MG	FIBER: 4 G	
CARBOHYDRATES: 65 G		SUGAR: 59 G

POMEGRANATE FOR PREVENTION

vegan, green, sweet

Providing the body with an astounding amount of vitamins, minerals, and powerful phytochemicals, pomegranate jewels not only add a ton of nutrition to every super smoothie, but also pack a punch of flavor! Combined with vitamin-K-rich spinach and potassium-rich bananas, this pomegranate smoothie is the perfect preventative measure.

18 OUNCES

½ cup pomegranate jewels
½ cup spinach
½ banana, peeled and frozen
1 cup green tea, cooled

1. In the 18-ounce NutriBullet cup, combine all ingredients.
2. Blend until all ingredients are thoroughly liquefied and combined, 30–60 seconds.
3. Consume immediately, or store with an airtight lid in the refrigerator for no more than 3–4 hours.

PER SERVING

CALORIES: 56	FAT: 0 G	PROTEIN: 1 G
SODIUM: 12 MG	FIBER: 2 G	
CARBOHYDRATES: 14 G		SUGAR: 7 G

CANTALOUPE CURE

vegan, green, sweet

Cantaloupe combines with deep green kale and sweet banana to provide your body with plentiful phytochemicals that promote health and well-being. Whether you need a calming cure for the common cold or hope to combat far more serious illnesses, the natural vitamins, minerals, and antioxidants that this super smoothie provides will fit the bill!

18 OUNCES

1 kale leaf

1 cup cantaloupe, rind and seeds removed

½ banana, peeled and frozen

1 cup purified water

1. In the 18-ounce NutriBullet cup, combine all ingredients.
2. Blend until all ingredients are thoroughly liquefied and combined, 30–60 seconds.
3. Consume immediately, or store with an airtight lid in the refrigerator for no more than 3–4 hours.

PER SERVING

CALORIES: 106	FAT: 0 G	PROTEIN: 2 G
SODIUM: 26 MG	FIBER: 3 G	
CARBOHYDRATES: 26 G		SUGAR: 20 G

BERRY BREATHE-EASY

vegan, sweet

Respiratory issues can be caused by a variety of conditions that range from acute allergies to symptoms stemming from serious illnesses. With anthocyanins that directly support the functioning of every aspect of the respiratory system, berries not only help you "breathe easy" but also provide ample amounts of vitamin C to promote the health of the entire body.

18 OUNCES

¼ cup blueberries
¼ cup blackberries
1 banana, peeled and frozen
1 cup green tea, cooled
¼" piece ginger, peeled

1. In the 18-ounce NutriBullet cup, combine all ingredients.
2. Blend until all ingredients are thoroughly liquefied and combined, 30–60 seconds.
3. Consume immediately, or store with an airtight lid in the refrigerator for no more than 3–4 hours.

PER SERVING

CALORIES: 142	FAT: 1 G	PROTEIN: 2 G
SODIUM: 2 MG	FIBER: 6 G	
CARBOHYDRATES: 36 G		SUGAR: 20 G

VITAMIN "C"ANCER PREVENTION

vegan, green, sweet

Simple citrus fruits contain vitamin C but don't receive credit for the essential antioxidants they provide. Helping to combat serious illness and disease, the vitamins, minerals, and phytochemicals of the citrus, spinach, and ginger make every sip of this super smoothie a step toward better health.

18 OUNCES

¼ cup spinach

½ medium red or pink grapefruit, peeled

¼ cup pineapple chunks

½ orange, peeled

¼" piece ginger, peeled

¾ cup purified water

1. In the 18-ounce NutriBullet cup, combine all ingredients.
2. Blend until all ingredients are thoroughly liquefied and combined, 30–60 seconds.
3. Consume immediately, or store with an airtight lid in the refrigerator for no more than 3–4 hours.

PER SERVING

CALORIES: 94	FAT: 0 G	PROTEIN: 2 G
SODIUM: 6 MG	FIBER: 2 G	
CARBOHYDRATES: 13 G		SUGAR: 10 G

Advanced Technology for Optimized Benefits

With patented extractor blades, the NutriBullet doesn't just develop superfoods into super-smooth super smoothies but actually unharnesses the maximum nutrition packed within their cells. Breaking through the membranes of cell walls, the NutriBullet's blades unleash the utmost nutrition for the ultimate benefits from your favorite super smoothies.

AYURVEDA CURE-ALL

vegan, green, sweet, paleo

The combination of ingredients in this super smoothie provides the body with essential vitamins, minerals, antioxidants, medium-chain fatty acids, and an abundance of phytochemicals that cure whatever ails you. Improving energy levels, mental focus, muscle maintenance, and bone health, all while optimizing the body's overall health, this super smoothie is a great addition to anyone's everyday routine.

18 OUNCES

¼ cup spinach
1 kale leaf
1 small Fuji apple, cored
1 large carrot, peeled and chopped
2 tablespoons aloe
1 tablespoon coconut oil
¼" piece ginger, peeled
1 cup purified water

1. In the 18-ounce NutriBullet cup, combine all ingredients.
2. Blend until all ingredients are thoroughly liquefied and combined, 30–60 seconds.
3. Consume immediately, or store with an airtight lid in the refrigerator for no more than 3–4 hours.

PER SERVING

CALORIES: 214	FAT: 14 G	PROTEIN: 1 G
SODIUM: 56 MG	FIBER: 2 G	
CARBOHYDRATES: 7 G		SUGAR: 3 G

SPICE IS NICE!

vegan, sweet, paleo

Not all sweet treats are bad for you. This super smoothie's sweetness comes from the rich flavors of sweet potato, carrot, and banana, only to be spiced even more with cinnamon and cloves, all whipped together with vanilla almond milk. This nutrient-dense sweet treat is the perfect healthy option for a snack or dessert any day of the week.

18 OUNCES

½ sweet potato, cleaned thoroughly, skin intact
1 carrot, chopped
½ banana, peeled and frozen
1 teaspoon ground organic cinnamon
½ teaspoon ground cloves
1 cup unsweetened vanilla almond milk

1. In the 18-ounce NutriBullet cup, combine all ingredients.
2. Blend until all ingredients are thoroughly liquefied and combined, 30–60 seconds.
3. Consume immediately, or store with an airtight lid in the refrigerator for no more than 3–4 hours.

PER SERVING

CALORIES: 147	FAT: 1 G	PROTEIN: 2 G
SODIUM: 89 MG	FIBER: 7 G	
CARBOHYDRATES: 36 G		SUGAR: 13 G

A, B, CS

sweet, paleo

The sweet combination of these vibrant flavors makes a creamy treat that provides astounding amounts of vitamins, minerals, antioxidants, and phytochemicals to protect the heart, eyes, muscles, and bones. Delicious and nutritious, this all-natural energizing super smoothie can be a kick-start in the morning or a jump-start in the afternoon.

18 OUNCES

1 Fuji apple, cored

1 large banana, peeled and frozen

1 large carrot, chopped

¼ teaspoon ground organic cinnamon

½ cup unsweetened vanilla almond milk

1. In the 18-ounce NutriBullet cup, combine all ingredients.
2. Blend until all ingredients are thoroughly liquefied and combined, 30–60 seconds.
3. Consume immediately, or store with an airtight lid in the refrigerator for no more than 3–4 hours.

PER SERVING

CALORIES: 249	FAT: 3 G	PROTEIN: 9 G
SODIUM: 164 MG	FIBER: 6 G	
CARBOHYDRATES: 51 G		SUGAR: 31 G

GO GREEN!

vegan, green, sweet

Vibrant leafy greens blend with sweet apple, pear, and kiwi into an antioxidant-rich green-tea super smoothie. These great green ingredients help ensure that the body receives all the vitamins and minerals it depends on, as well as a healthy dose of protective antioxidants to prevent illness and disease.

18 OUNCES

½ cup spinach

¼ teaspoon spirulina

1 large kale leaf

1 kiwi

½ Granny Smith apple, cored

½ green pear, cored

½ cup green tea, cooled

1. In the 18-ounce NutriBullet cup, combine all ingredients.
2. Blend until all ingredients are thoroughly liquefied and combined, 30–60 seconds.
3. Consume immediately, or store with an airtight lid in the refrigerator for no more than 3–4 hours.

PER SERVING

CALORIES: 98	FAT: 0 G	PROTEIN: 1 G
SODIUM: 16 MG	FIBER: 5 G	
CARBOHYDRATES: 25 G		SUGAR: 8 G

SWEET, SPICY SIMPLICITY

vegan, green, sweet

The surprising combination of sweet pears with sea algae and apple cider vinegar creates a taste sensation while delivering on powerful vitamins, minerals, and phytochemicals that support the body's needs and protect against illness and disease.

18 OUNCES

½ teaspoon spirulina

2 Bartlett pears, cored

¼" piece ginger, peeled

1 tablespoon organic, unfiltered, unpasteurized apple cider vinegar

1 cup green tea, cooled

1. In the 18-ounce NutriBullet cup, combine all ingredients.
2. Blend until all ingredients are thoroughly liquefied and combined, 30–60 seconds.
3. Consume immediately, or store with an airtight lid in the refrigerator for no more than 3–4 hours.

PER SERVING

CALORIES: 193	FAT: 0 G	PROTEIN: 1 G
SODIUM: 4 MG	FIBER: 10 G	
CARBOHYDRATES: 51 G		SUGAR: 33 G

CHAPTER 3

14 SMOOTHIES FOR WEIGHT LOSS

Millions of people engage in a never-ending struggle with weight loss. If even a fraction of the billions of dollars spent on weight-loss products every year was spent on fresh produce, fruit, nuts, and seeds, we'd see real progress in the fight against obesity. These items can be easily combined in a NutriBullet, producing delicious and nutritious smoothies that benefit the entire body with their rich sources of vitamins, minerals, and unique phytochemicals.

NutriBullet smoothies in this chapter boost the fat-burning potential of the metabolism while encouraging proper use of the natural fats and carbohydrates in each smoothie. As a result, the metabolic functioning (and every process with which it is involved) is optimized. These delicious super smoothies are packed with the precise nutrients any body needs to achieve or maintain weight loss, can be consumed as either a snack or a meal, and are prepared quickly enough to meet anyone's scheduling demands. Delicious, nutritious, fast, and easy, these super smoothies make weight loss simple!

METABOLISM MAXIMIZER

vegan, green, sweet

Supporting the circulatory system, digestive system, and metabolism, this super smoothie sparks a fire within the body for maximized fat-burning potential. With sweet apple, cool cucumber, crisp kale, and a dash of spicy cayenne, this smoothie provides fiber-filled nutrition for a burst of thermogenic energy.

18 OUNCES

½ large Fuji apple, cored
1 stalk celery, with leaves
½ cucumber
¼ teaspoon spirulina
1 cup green tea, cooled

1. In the 18-ounce NutriBullet cup, combine all ingredients.
2. Blend until all ingredients are thoroughly liquefied and combined, 30–60 seconds.
3. Consume immediately, or store with an airtight lid in the refrigerator for no more than 3–4 hours.

PER SERVING

CALORIES: 29	FAT: 0 G	PROTEIN: 1 G
SODIUM: 35 MG	FIBER: 1 G	
CARBOHYDRATES: 7 G		SUGAR: 3 G

FEROCIOUS FIVE-POUND FIGHTER

vegan, green, sweet

Everybody knows the "ferocious five-pound" dilemma that stalls the achievement of weight-loss success. This craving-calming combination of hydrating, low-calorie, high-fiber foods fights those last few pounds and makes for a sweet super smoothie that provides the body with metabolism-boosting support and a satisfied sense of fullness, helping to maintain weight loss and achieve success.

18 OUNCES

½ cup spinach leaves

½ large Fuji apple, cored

½ cucumber

½ stalk celery

1 cup organic apple juice (see Introduction)

1. In the 18-ounce NutriBullet cup, combine all ingredients.
2. Blend until all ingredients are thoroughly liquefied and combined, 30–60 seconds.
3. Consume immediately, or store with an airtight lid in the refrigerator for no more than 3–4 hours.

PER SERVING

CALORIES: 143	FAT: 1 G	PROTEIN: 2 G
SODIUM: 41 MG	FIBER: 2 G	
CARBOHYDRATES: 35 G		SUGAR: 27 G

MIGHTY MELON-CITRUS

vegan, sweet

A super smoothie that combines cantaloupe, honeydew, orange, and grapefruit is not only delightfully delicious, but can help anyone achieve weight-loss success. With filling fiber, the melons and citrus fruits support the functioning of the systems that contribute to healthy weight management. Providing vitamins, minerals, phytochemicals, and fiber, this colorful combination of hydrating ingredients will not just keep pounds off but will optimize health in every area imaginable.

18 OUNCES

½ cup cantaloupe
½ cup honeydew
½ orange, rind intact
½ grapefruit, rind intact
¼ cup organic apple juice (see Introduction)

1. In the 18-ounce NutriBullet cup, combine all ingredients.
2. Blend until all ingredients are thoroughly liquefied and combined, 30–60 seconds.
3. Consume immediately, or store with an airtight lid in the refrigerator for no more than 3–4 hours.

PER SERVING

CALORIES: 127	FAT: 0 G	PROTEIN: 2 G
SODIUM: 15 MG	FIBER: 4 G	
CARBOHYDRATES: 31 G		SUGAR: 27 G

SWEET GREEN APPLE-PEAR

vegan, green, sweet

Packed with antioxidant-rich fiber-filled ingredients, this smoothie not only improves health but also calms cravings, minimizes munching, and eliminates the urge to binge on unhealthy foods. It provides the perfect balance of essential dietary servings and delectable deliciousness.

18 OUNCES

½ cup spinach

1 large kale leaf

½ medium Granny Smith apple, cored

½ medium Bartlett pear, cored

½ cup green tea, cooled

1. In the 18-ounce NutriBullet cup, combine all ingredients.
2. Blend until all ingredients are thoroughly liquefied and combined, 30–60 seconds.
3. Consume immediately, or store with an airtight lid in the refrigerator for no more than 3–4 hours.

PER SERVING

CALORIES: 69	FAT: 0 G	PROTEIN: 2 G
SODIUM: 24 MG	FIBER: 4 G	
CARBOHYDRATES: 17 G		SUGAR: 9 G

SKINNY SENSATION

vegan, green, sweet

This sensational super smoothie combines fiber-rich fruits and veggies that not only help rid the body of toxins and waste but support the metabolism. Through rich provisions of vitamins, minerals, and phytochemicals, the spinach, apple, pear, and ginger create the perfect slimming super smoothie that helps you lose weight, feel great, and live healthfully!

18 OUNCES

½ cup spinach
½ Fuji apple, cored
½ pear, cored
¼" piece ginger, peeled
1 cup green tea, cooled

1. In the 18-ounce NutriBullet cup, combine all ingredients.
2. Blend until all ingredients are thoroughly liquefied and combined, 30–60 seconds.
3. Consume immediately, or store with an airtight lid in the refrigerator for no more than 3–4 hours.

PER SERVING

CALORIES: 90	FAT: 0 G	PROTEIN: 1 G
SODIUM: 13 MG	FIBER: 4 G	
CARBOHYDRATES: 23 G		SUGAR: 16 G

CUCUMBER COOLER

vegan, green, sweet, paleo

With only four simple ingredients, this super smoothie combines hydrating, nutrient-dense fruits and greens with refreshing coconut milk for a light-tasting snack or meal that promotes energy levels and improves metabolism functioning. Nutritious and delicious, this super smoothie's nutrients and phytochemicals help to achieve and maintain optimal levels of health throughout the entire body.

18 OUNCES

1 large English cucumber, halved and chopped

½ cup spinach, chopped

½ cup pineapple chunks

1 cup unsweetened vanilla coconut milk

1. In the 18-ounce NutriBullet cup, combine all ingredients.
2. Blend until all ingredients are thoroughly liquefied and combined, 30–60 seconds.
3. Consume immediately, or store with an airtight lid in the refrigerator for no more than 3–4 hours.

PER SERVING

CALORIES: 189	FAT: 4 G	PROTEIN: 9 G
SODIUM: 113 MG	FIBER: 4 G	
CARBOHYDRATES: 32 G		SUGAR: 20 G

WEIGHT-LOSS SUCCESS

vegan, green, sweet

With deeply colored greens, bright red beets, beautiful apples and bananas, and green tea, this fiber-filled concoction is a sweet treat that helps keep the body clean, focused, and fit. These powerful nutrients promote the health of the blood, digestive system, and brain, helping anyone achieve weight-loss success and optimize overall health.

18 OUNCES

¼ cup beet greens
1 small red beet, chopped
1 small Fuji apple, cored
½ banana, peeled and frozen
1 cup green tea, cooled

1. In the 18-ounce NutriBullet cup, combine all ingredients.
2. Blend until all ingredients are thoroughly liquefied and combined, 30–60 seconds.
3. Consume immediately, or store with an airtight lid in the refrigerator for no more than 3–4 hours.

PER SERVING

CALORIES: 165	FAT: 1 G	PROTEIN: 3 G
SODIUM: 91 MG	FIBER: 6 G	
CARBOHYDRATES: 41 G		SUGAR: 28 G

BLUE JUICE

vegan, sweet, paleo

Berries take center stage in this super smoothie to provide a blend of polyphenols that have been shown to stimulate the brain, improve energy, and keep the body free of illness. Medium-chain fatty acids from the aloe and coconut oil further improve the benefits to metabolic functioning, muscle maintenance, and fat loss.

18 OUNCES

½ cup blueberries
½ cup blackberries
1 tablespoon aloe vera juice
1 tablespoon coconut oil
1 cup green tea, cooled

1. In the 18-ounce NutriBullet cup, combine all ingredients.
2. Blend until all ingredients are thoroughly liquefied and combined, 30–60 seconds.
3. Consume immediately, or store with an airtight lid in the refrigerator for no more than 3–4 hours.

PER SERVING

CALORIES: 193	FAT: 14 G	PROTEIN: 2 G
SODIUM: 1 MG	FIBER: 6 G	
CARBOHYDRATES: 18 G		SUGAR: 11 G

FILLING FIBER

vegan, green, sweet

With a heavy dose of fiber-filled fruits and vegetables, this filling super smoothie packs a punch for weight loss by filling you up without weighing you down. Cleansing the body of toxins, improving the metabolism's functioning, and protecting the body's systems from illness and disease, these antioxidant-rich delights combine for a sweet treat that helps anyone lose weight, feel great, and achieve optimal health!

18 OUNCES

1 small Fuji apple, cored

1 small Bartlett pear, cored

1 kale leaf

¼ cup blueberries

1 cup green tea, cooled

1. In the 18-ounce NutriBullet cup, combine all ingredients.
2. Blend until all ingredients are thoroughly liquefied and combined, 30–60 seconds.
3. Consume immediately, or store with an airtight lid in the refrigerator for no more than 3–4 hours.

PER SERVING

CALORIES: 21	FAT: 0 G	PROTEIN: 0 G
SODIUM: 0 MG	FIBER: 1 G	
CARBOHYDRATES: 5 G		SUGAR: 4 G

WONDERS OF WATERMELON

vegan, green, sweet

Watermelon and mint pair for a taste sensation that refreshes, hydrates, and energizes. Naturally packed with protein, vitamins, minerals, and phytochemicals, this super smoothie promotes energy levels, maintains muscle mass, and cleanses the body of impurities. This wonderful watermelon super smoothie is a natural wonder for achieving weight-loss success and is a perfect treat for any time of day!

18 OUNCES

2 cups watermelon, cubed
½ cup spinach
2 tablespoons chopped fresh mint

1. In the 18-ounce NutriBullet cup, combine all ingredients.
2. Blend until all ingredients are thoroughly liquefied and combined, 30–60 seconds.
3. Consume immediately, or store with an airtight lid in the refrigerator for no more than 3–4 hours.

PER SERVING

CALORIES: 100	FAT: 1 G	PROTEIN: 3 G
SODIUM: 18 MG	FIBER: 2 G	
CARBOHYDRATES: 24 G		SUGAR: 19 G

SWEET CITRUS CINCHER

vegan, sweet

With four sweet and tangy fruits combined in one super smoothie, this sweet treat is a delicious way to sip yourself slim. The benefits are endless—vitamin C, magnesium, and plenty of phytochemicals that promote healthy system functioning. Maximizing metabolism, enhancing energy levels, and supporting and sustaining weight loss, this fiber-filled combo will keep you satisfied in every way.

18 OUNCES

½ orange, peeled
1 small tangerine, peeled
¼ cup red or pink grapefruit
¼ cup pineapple chunks
¼ cup water

1. In the 18-ounce NutriBullet cup, combine all ingredients.
2. Blend until all ingredients are thoroughly liquefied and combined, 30–60 seconds.
3. Consume immediately, or store with an airtight lid in the refrigerator for no more than 3–4 hours.

PER SERVING

CALORIES: 92	FAT: 0 G	PROTEIN: 1 G
SODIUM: 2 MG	FIBER: 4 G	
CARBOHYDRATES: 23 G		SUGAR: 18 G

APPLE PIE

vegan, green, sweet, paleo

With the sensational tastiness of apple pie, this super smoothie combines the nutrients of greens and quercetin-rich apples with the creaminess of blended cashews and spicy cinnamon and cloves. The result is a boost for your immune system. Packed with fiber and antioxidants that keep your body clear of toxins and protected from illness, this super smoothie is a sweet treat you can enjoy without guilt.

18 OUNCES

1 Granny Smith apple, cored

½ cup spinach

1 ounce cashews

1 teaspoon ground organic cinnamon

½ teaspoon cloves

1 cup vanilla almond milk

1. In the 18-ounce NutriBullet cup, combine all ingredients.
2. Blend until all ingredients are thoroughly liquefied and combined, 30–60 seconds.
3. Consume immediately, or store with an airtight lid in the refrigerator for no more than 3–4 hours.

PER SERVING

CALORIES: 112	FAT: 4 G	PROTEIN: 7 G
SODIUM: 109 MG	FIBER: 3 G	
CARBOHYDRATES: 13 G		SUGAR: 7 G

KIWI-MELON FOR MAINTENANCE

vegan, sweet

The vitamins, minerals, and phytochemicals in this all-natural treat provide the body with the nutrition it needs to stay fit and focused. At the same time, they improve the functioning of every system . . . especially the immune system. With increased energy, improved cognitive functioning, and optimized protection against illness, this vitamin-C-packed super smoothie is a treat that does it all.

18 OUNCES

1 kiwi

1 cup cubed cantaloupe

1 cup cubed honeydew

½ banana, peeled and frozen

1 cup purified water

1. In the 18-ounce NutriBullet cup, combine all ingredients except water.
2. Blend until all ingredients are thoroughly liquefied and combined, 30–60 seconds.
3. Add water gradually while blending until desired consistency is achieved.
4. Consume immediately, or store with an airtight lid in the refrigerator for no more than 3–4 hours.

PER SERVING

CALORIES: 213	FAT: 1 G	PROTEIN: 4 G
SODIUM: 60 MG	FIBER: 7 G	
CARBOHYDRATES: 53 G		SUGAR: 33 G

FIT AND FIBERFUL

vegan, green, sweet

Apple, pear, kale, cantaloupe, and ginger combine in this super smoothie to create a sweet and slightly spiced blend of refreshment that hydrates the body's cells, removes toxins and waste, and maximizes metabolism. Through their vibrant provisions of nutrients, phytochemicals, and antioxidants, these foods keep you feeling full, energized, and focused, helping you set and achieve any weight-related goal.

18 OUNCES

1 Fuji apple, cored
½ Bartlett pear, cored
1 kale leaf
1 cup cantaloupe
¼" piece ginger, peeled
1 cup purified water

1. In the 18-ounce NutriBullet cup, combine all ingredients except water.
2. Blend until all ingredients are thoroughly liquefied and combined, 30–60 seconds.
3. Add water gradually while blending until desired consistency is achieved.
4. Consume immediately, or store with an airtight lid in the refrigerator for no more than 3–4 hours.

PER SERVING

CALORIES: 53	FAT: 0 G	PROTEIN: 1 G
SODIUM: 25 MG	FIBER: 1 G	
CARBOHYDRATES: 13 G		SUGAR: 12 G

CHAPTER 4

13 SMOOTHIES THAT CLEANSE AND DETOX YOUR BODY

Cleansing and detoxification have never been more popular than they are today. And the science is in: Numerous studies have determined that detox and cleansing are beneficial for your digestive tract, immune system functioning, metabolism, and brain functioning. The cleansing combinations of specific groups of fruits, vegetables, and additions benefit the body's detoxification processes. The NutriBullet's design can help you transform the most nutrient-dense smoothie into one that is easily absorbed and readily available to the body's most intricate systems and functions, providing the body with nutrients that are biochemically available for use as soon as they enter the mouth, digestive system, and bloodstream. These delicious and nutritious combinations not only provide your body with the precise phytochemicals needed for maximum detoxification and purification, but also support the body's needs for restorative balance, allowing for maximum benefit to every aspect of health and functioning!

DELICIOUS DETOX

vegan, sweet

There's never been a more delicious way to detox than with this super smoothie packed with berries, bananas, and green tea. Helping to rid the body of harsh chemicals while providing antioxidant support, this beautiful blend of ingredients purifies the body with every sweet and splendid sip!

18 OUNCES

¼ cup strawberries
¼ cup blueberries
1 medium banana
¼" piece ginger, peeled
1 cup green tea, cooled

1. In the 18-ounce NutriBullet cup, combine all ingredients.
2. Blend until all ingredients are thoroughly liquefied and combined, 30–60 seconds.
3. Consume immediately, or store with an airtight lid in the refrigerator for no more than 3–4 hours.

PER SERVING

CALORIES: 123	FAT: 1 G	PROTEIN: 2 G
SODIUM: 2 MG	FIBER: 4 G	
CARBOHYDRATES: 31 G		SUGAR: 18 G

QUICK CARROT CLEANSE

sweet

Beta-carotene, a powerful antioxidant that helps support immune system functioning, enhances this probiotic-rich blend that purges toxins and replenishes good bacteria in the digestive system. Through its provisions of vitamins, minerals, and phytochemicals, this smoothie purifies your body and protects your health.

18 OUNCES

1 large carrot, peeled and end removed, chopped
1 large Fuji apple, cored
1 tablespoon ground flax seed
1 teaspoon ground organic cinnamon
½ cup low-fat kefir
½ cup flax milk

1. In the 18-ounce NutriBullet cup, combine all ingredients.
2. Blend until all ingredients are thoroughly liquefied and combined, 30–60 seconds.
3. Consume immediately, or store with an airtight lid in the refrigerator for no more than 3–4 hours.

PER SERVING

CALORIES: 470	FAT: 30 G	PROTEIN: 10 G
SODIUM: 120 MG	FIBER: 8 G	
CARBOHYDRATES: 47 G		SUGAR: 20 G
SUGAR: 30 G		

SPICY PEAR PURIFIER

vegan, green, sweet

The sweet and spicy combination of pears and ginger makes every detoxifying sip of this super smoothie that much more splendid! Providing cleansing fiber, immunity-boosting antioxidants, and a rich supply of nutrients that support the systems responsible for ridding the body of impurities, this super smoothie is a delicious and powerful dietary addition.

18 OUNCES

½ cup spinach
1 large Bartlett pear, cored
¼" piece ginger, peeled
1 cup green tea, cooled

1. In the 18-ounce NutriBullet cup, combine all ingredients.
2. Blend until all ingredients are thoroughly liquefied and combined, 30–60 seconds.
3. Consume immediately, or store with an airtight lid in the refrigerator for no more than 3–4 hours.

PER SERVING

CALORIES: 137	FAT: 0 G	PROTEIN: 1 G
SODIUM: 14 MG	FIBER: 7 G	
CARBOHYDRATES: 36 G		SUGAR: 23 G

BEET THE BLOAT

vegan, green, sweet, paleo

Excessive water retention stands no chance when this smoothie is put into play. With vibrant, nutrient-dense beets, beet greens, Fuji apples, and ginger that help rid the body of toxins and combat the effects of the additives in processed foods, this super smoothie succeeds in beating thc bloat with delicious nutrition that improves health and appearance!

18 OUNCES

1 red beet, greens removed, chopped

½ cup of the rinsed and chopped beet greens

½ large Fuji apple, cored

¼" piece ginger, peeled

1 cup organic apple juice (see Introduction)

1. In the 18-ounce NutriBullet cup, combine all ingredients.
2. Blend until all ingredients are thoroughly liquefied and combined, 30–60 seconds.
3. Consume immediately, or store with an airtight lid in the refrigerator for no more than 3–4 hours.

PER SERVING

CALORIES: 230	FAT: 1 G	PROTEIN: 3 G
SODIUM: 126 MG	FIBER: 6 G	
CARBOHYDRATES: 56 G		SUGAR: 45 G

CLEANSING CUCUMBER CARROT

vegan, sweet, paleo

With flavors of sweet carrots and apple combined with the naturally refreshing flavor of cucumber, this super smoothie provides not only a healthy dose of cleansing fiber but also a taste that makes it a delectable treat. This smoothie helps remove toxins and expel waste to achieve and maintain a clean and healthy digestive system that can function at its best!

18 OUNCES

2 large carrots, peeled and chopped

2 medium cucumbers

½ medium Fuji apple, cored

1 cup purified water

1. In the 18-ounce NutriBullet cup, combine all ingredients.
2. Blend until all ingredients are thoroughly liquefied and combined, 30–60 seconds.
3. Consume immediately, or store with an airtight lid in the refrigerator for no more than 3–4 hours.

PER SERVING

CALORIES: 187	FAT: 1 G	PROTEIN: 5 G
SODIUM: 111 MG	FIBER: 84 G	
CARBOHYDRATES: 46 G		SUGAR: 25 G

SWEET SPINACH

vegan, green, sweet, paleo

The fiber-rich ingredients in this super smoothie combine to create the perfect healthy helping of cleansing nutrition to restore a better balance to any body. The fiber, antioxidants, vitamins A, C, E, and K, along with iron, calcium, and magnesium provide the body's systems and cells with everything they need to be fit and healthy.

18 OUNCES

½ cup spinach
½ Granny Smith apple, cored
½ Bartlett pear, cored
1 kiwi
1 cup purified water

1. In the 18-ounce NutriBullet cup, combine all ingredients.
2. Blend until all ingredients are thoroughly liquefied and combined, 30–60 seconds.
3. Consume immediately, or store with an airtight lid in the refrigerator for no more than 3–4 hours.

PER SERVING

CALORIES: 97	FAT: 0 G	PROTEIN: 1 G
SODIUM: 16 MG	FIBER: 5 G	
CARBOHYDRATES: 25 G		SUGAR: 8 G

BERRY-BANANA BLEND

sweet

Berries and bananas have long been combined for a tasty treat, but this super smoothie makes their tastes even more sensational! Blended with creamy almond milk, this super smoothie packs a variety of vital nutrients into every last sip. Helping to deliver essential nutrients such as protein, B vitamins, potassium, and protein throughout the body, this berry-banana blend is simply blissful!

18 OUNCES

¼ cup strawberries
¼ cup blueberries
1 banana, peeled and frozen
1 cup vanilla almond milk

1. In the 18-ounce NutriBullet cup, combine all ingredients.
2. Blend until all ingredients are thoroughly liquefied and combined, 30–60 seconds.
3. Consume immediately, or store with an airtight lid in the refrigerator for no more than 3–4 hours.

PER SERVING

CALORIES: 187	FAT: 2 G	PROTEIN: 5 G
SODIUM: 49 MG	FIBER: 5 G	
CARBOHYDRATES: 40 G		SUGAR: 23 G

COOL BLUE CANTALOUPE CLEANSE

vegan, green, sweet

Sweet cantaloupe gets even sweeter with the additions of blueberries and blackberries. Fiber-filled, hydrating cantaloupe and berries combine with the green tea, making this super smoothie an antioxidant-rich, polyphenol-filled snack or meal that rids the body of toxins and waste while supporting the immune system and protecting against illness and disease.

18 OUNCES

½ cup blueberries
½ cup blackberries
¼ teaspoon spirulina
½ cup cantaloupe, cubed
1 cup green tea, cooled

1. In the 18-ounce NutriBullet cup, combine all ingredients.
2. Blend until all ingredients are thoroughly liquefied and combined, 30–60 seconds.
3. Consume immediately, or store with an airtight lid in the refrigerator for no more than 3–4 hours.

PER SERVING

CALORIES: 100	FAT: 1 G	PROTEIN: 2 G
SODIUM: 14 MG	FIBER: 6 G	
CARBOHYDRATES: 24 G		SUGAR: 17 G

Simple Spirulina for Maximum Benefits
With this simple addition, you can introduce one of the most bioavailable protein-packed ingredients to your super smoothies! Spirulina has abundant antioxidants and plenty of plant-based protein that will improve the nutrition content of your favorite smoothies with little or no taste change.

BERRY BEET TREAT

vegan, sweet, paleo

Beautiful berries and deep-golden beets combine with apple in this super smoothie that helps cleanse, detoxify, refresh, and restore. With polyphenols that help to purge the body's digestive and respiratory systems of potentially harmful toxins, the berries join forces with antioxidant-rich apples for a fiber-filled combination that rids the body of waste and restores a natural balance.

18 OUNCES

½ cup blueberries

½ cup raspberries

½ golden beet, greens removed, chopped

½ Fuji apple, cored

1 cup purified water

1. In the 18-ounce NutriBullet cup, combine all ingredients.
2. Blend until all ingredients are thoroughly liquefied and combined, 30–60 seconds.
3. Consume immediately, or store with an airtight lid in the refrigerator for no more than 3–4 hours.

PER SERVING

CALORIES: 92	FAT: 1 G	PROTEIN: 2 G
SODIUM: 33 MG	FIBER: 7 G	
CARBOHYDRATES: 22 G		SUGAR: 13 G

APPLE AND SPICE

vegan, sweet, paleo

Apples take center stage in this super smoothie. This recipe optimizes the effectiveness of the naturally occurring antioxidants in apples together with the antioxidant-rich spices cinnamon and cloves. Accentuated by enzyme-packed ginger, this blend of delicious ingredients makes for a nutrient-dense snack or meal that's light and refreshing enough to enjoy any time.

18 OUNCES

2 Fuji apples, cored

½ teaspoons ground organic cinnamon

¼ teaspoon ground cloves

¼" piece ginger, peeled

1 cup purified water

1. In the 18-ounce NutriBullet cup, combine all ingredients.

2. Blend until all ingredients are thoroughly liquefied and combined, 30–60 seconds.

3. Consume immediately, or store with an airtight lid in the refrigerator for no more than 3–4 hours.

PER SERVING

CALORIES: 159	FAT: 1 G	PROTEIN: 1 G
SODIUM: 1 MG	FIBER: 5 G	
CARBOHYDRATES: 42 G		SUGAR: 32 G

HANGOVER HEALER

vegan, sweet, paleo

A lingering "less-than-healthy" feeling can result from any overindulgence. To restore a healthy, happy, fit, and focused balance, this super smoothie provides abundant vitamins, minerals, fiber, and natural phytochemicals that deliver healing help to the brain, digestive system, blood, muscles, and nerves. When these areas of the body are replenished with restored nutrients, you're well on your way to a healthier, happier you!

18 OUNCES

1 medium cucumber

½ medium red or pink grapefruit

½ tangerine, peeled

1 kiwi

½ cup purified water

1. In the 18-ounce NutriBullet cup, combine all ingredients.
2. Blend until all ingredients are thoroughly liquefied and combined, 30–60 seconds.
3. Consume immediately, or store with an airtight lid in the refrigerator for no more than 3–4 hours.

PER SERVING

CALORIES: 75	FAT: 1 G	PROTEIN: 1 G
SODIUM: 5 MG	FIBER: 4 G	
CARBOHYDRATES: 19 G		SUGAR: 5 G

GREAT "GREEN" GREEN TEA

vegan, green, sweet

With fiber, vitamin K, vitamin C, B vitamins, protein, iron, and an abundance of phytochemicals, this super smoothie's delicious blend of nutrient-dense foods makes for a sweet treat that can be enjoyed morning, noon, or night . . . helping to detoxify and cleanse naturally.

18 OUNCES

¼ cup spinach
1 large kale leaf
1 Fuji apple, cored
½ Bartlett pear, cored
1 cup green tea, cooled

1. In the 18-ounce NutriBullet cup, combine all ingredients.
2. Blend until all ingredients are thoroughly liquefied and combined, 30–60 seconds.
3. Consume immediately, or store with an airtight lid in the refrigerator for no more than 3–4 hours.

PER SERVING

CALORIES: 169	FAT: 1 G	PROTEIN: 4 G
SODIUM: 42 MG	FIBER: 7 G	
CARBOHYDRATES: 42 G		SUGAR: 24 G

KEEP IT CLEAN!

vegan, sweet

There's no sweeter way to detoxify your body than with fruits rich in fiber, antioxidants, vitamins, minerals, and powerful phytochemicals that cleanse the digestive system, support the immune system, and replenish the body's stores of essential nutrients. This super smoothie is a tasty aid to cleaner, healthier living!

18 OUNCES

1 Fuji apple, cored
1 Bartlett pear, cored
1 banana, peeled and frozen
¼" piece ginger, peeled
1 cup green tea, cooled

1. In the 18-ounce NutriBullet cup, combine all ingredients.
2. Blend until all ingredients are thoroughly liquefied and combined, 30–60 seconds.
3. Consume immediately, or store with an airtight lid in the refrigerator for no more than 3–4 hours.

PER SERVING

CALORIES: 278	FAT: 1 G	PROTEIN: 2 G
SODIUM: 3 MG	FIBER: 10 G	
CARBOHYDRATES: 73 G		SUGAR: 47 G

The Value of Clean Eating

When you base your diet on a variety of natural foods, you can keep your diet clean and clear of processed, sugar- and sodium-laden foods full of unhealthy fats and unnatural ingredients. Providing your body with rich all-natural superfoods that pack tons of nutrition into every flavorful bite gives your body what it needs, with protective antioxidants and phytochemicals that safeguard and optimize health deliciously!

CHAPTER 5

14 SMOOTHIES FOR BETTER DIGESTIVE HEALTH

Few people are aware of the profound impact the gut's health can have on the entire body. Many people fail to realize that the digestive system is responsible for the absorption of essential nutrients from foods. It regulates and disperses a variety of hormones and facilitates numerous enzymatic reactions. To care for this system and ensure that it performs at its best, you must provide it with the nutrition it needs to maintain proper functioning. You should consume foods that not only supply proper nutrition but also contribute the essential fiber content needed to keep this system running smoothly.

With a variety of tasty fruits, vegetables, and additions that promote the health of the digestive system, these super smoothies will support the everyday functions of the system and ensure that fiber, vitamins A, C, and E, and a variety of essential minerals are readily available for use. Through the cleansing process, potentially harmful waste is removed from your body. Through the supply of antioxidants, your digestion helps suppress illnesses and disease. Through the delivery of essential nutrients, the system supports the entire body, delivering the means for a better functioning gut, an optimally functioning body, and greater overall health.

COLITIS-CALMING CARROT-CITRUS-APPLE

sweet, paleo

Sweet fruits and vegetables, along with protein-packed kefir, provide a troubled digestive system with fiber, a wide array of nutrients, and soothing protein. This colitis-calming blend of a super smoothie will help anyone troubled with digestive issues achieve a better balance in the gut and improve his or her colitis condition for good!

18 OUNCES

½ Granny Smith apple, cored

2 medium carrots, peeled and ends removed, chopped

1 kiwi

½ cup vanilla almond milk

½ cup purified water

1. In the 18-ounce NutriBullet cup, combine all ingredients except the water.
2. Blend until all ingredients are thoroughly liquefied and combined, 30–60 seconds.
3. Add water gradually while blending until desired consistency is achieved.
4. Consume immediately, or store with an airtight lid in the refrigerator for no more than 3–4 hours.

PER SERVING

CALORIES: 141	FAT: 1 G	PROTEIN: 3 G
SODIUM: 88 MG	FIBER: 7 G	
CARBOHYDRATES: 34 G		SUGAR: 15 G

FIBERFUL FANTASIA

vegan, green, sweet

With every ingredient in this super smoothie providing fiber, this sweet treat is the most enjoyable way to sip yourself to smoother digestion and regularity. The phytochemicals and phytonutrients in this smoothie help to achieve and maintain optimal digestive health by cleansing the digestive tract, improving the functioning of every organ involved in digestion, and maintaining an optimal balance of beneficial bacteria.

18 OUNCES

1 kiwi

1 Bartlett pear, cored

1 banana, peeled and frozen

½ cup spinach

1 cup green tea, cooled

1. In the 18-ounce NutriBullet cup, combine all ingredients.
2. Blend until all ingredients are thoroughly liquefied and combined, 30–60 seconds.
3. Consume immediately, or store with an airtight lid in the refrigerator for no more than 3–4 hours.

PER SERVING

CALORIES: 251	FAT: 1 G	PROTEIN: 3 G
SODIUM: 18 MG	FIBER: 11 G	
CARBOHYDRATES: 64 G		SUGAR: 31 G

Fiber for Benefits

When you introduce fiber-rich fruits and veggies to your daily diet, you help every aspect of your digestive system. Because that system houses the majority of your immune system, the benefits to your body are infinite! With the cleansing gel that's produced from fibrous produce, you can cleanse your colon and improve nutrient absorption and immune system functioning.

SWEET CITRUS-PEAR

vegan, green, sweet, paleo

Packed with fiber, vitamin C, vitamin K, quercetin, and antioxidants, this super smoothie is an excellent way to improve the digestive system's health and maintain effective immunity. With sweet citrus ingredients, vibrant greens, and soothing apple juice, this recipe sends valuable nutrients directly to the digestive system and throughout the entire body.

18 OUNCES

¼ cup spinach

1 medium red grapefruit

1 Bartlett pear, cored

1 kiwi

1 cup organic apple juice (see Introduction)

1. In the 18-ounce NutriBullet cup, combine all ingredients.
2. Blend until all ingredients are thoroughly liquefied and combined, 30–60 seconds.
3. Consume immediately, or store with an airtight lid in the refrigerator for no more than 3–4 hours.

PER SERVING

CALORIES: 244	FAT: 1 G	PROTEIN: 3 G
SODIUM: 20 MG	FIBER: 6 G	
CARBOHYDRATES: 60 G		SUGAR: 42 G

Picking the Perfect Pear

With pears adding potent antioxidants, phytochemicals, and fiber into your delicious super smoothies, it's important to know how to pick the perfect ones. A firm pear that has a subtle "give" close to the stem and the area around it is the ripest, most nutritious fruit. Steer clear of overly firm or mushy pears; their immature or overripe flesh yields lower nutrient content and can be less flavorful.

BELLY BLEND

vegan, sweet, paleo

Soothing berries, banana, and kiwi get blended into a super smoothie that provides the belly with flushing fiber, restorative vitamins and minerals, and reparative phytochemicals. All of these protect and support the health of the digestive system and all its functions.

18 OUNCES

½ cup strawberries
½ cup blueberries
1 banana, peeled and frozen
1 kiwi
1 cup organic apple juice (see Introduction)

1. In the 18-ounce NutriBullet cup, combine all ingredients.
2. Blend until all ingredients are thoroughly liquefied and combined, 30–60 seconds.
3. Consume immediately, or store with an airtight lid in the refrigerator for no more than 3–4 hours.

PER SERVING

CALORIES: 330	FAT: 2 G	PROTEIN: 3 G
SODIUM: 16 MG	FIBER: 9 G	
CARBOHYDRATES: 83 G		SUGAR: 49 G

MANGO-MELON MENDER

vegan, sweet

Light and refreshing, this mango-melon blend combines with antioxidant-rich green tea for a sweet and simple culinary concoction that supports the health of the entire digestive system. Whether the tummy trouble is slight discomfort, constipation, or diarrhea, this super smoothie provides the precise nutrients and antioxidants that mend all.

18 OUNCES

1 cup mango
½ cup cubed cantaloupe
½ cup cubed honeydew
1 cup green tea, cooled

1. In the 18-ounce NutriBullet cup, combine all ingredients.
2. Blend until all ingredients are thoroughly liquefied and combined, 30–60 seconds.
3. Consume immediately, or store with an airtight lid in the refrigerator for no more than 3–4 hours.

PER SERVING

CALORIES: 164	FAT: 1 G	PROTEIN: 2 G
SODIUM: 31 MG	FIBER: 4 G	
CARBOHYDRATES: 42 G		SUGAR: 37 G

PERFECT PAPAYA PREVENTION

sweet

Vibrant papaya combines with sweet pear, banana, and kefir for a nutrient-packed super smoothie of pure pleasure. Vitamin A, beta-carotene, fiber, and probiotics come together in this sweet treat to provide the tummy with preventative and supportive nutrients that help to achieve regularity, optimal health, and protection against illness and disease.

18 OUNCES

½ cup papaya
1 Bartlett pear, cored
1 banana, peeled and frozen
½ cup nonfat vanilla kefir
½ cup red raspberry tea

1. In the 18-ounce NutriBullet cup, combine all ingredients.
2. Blend until all ingredients are thoroughly liquefied and combined, 30–60 seconds.
3. Consume immediately, or store with an airtight lid in the refrigerator for no more than 3–4 hours.

PER SERVING

CALORIES: 234	FAT: 1 G	PROTEIN: 3 G
SODIUM: 6 MG	FIBER: 10 G	
CARBOHYDRATES: 61 G		SUGAR: 36 G

CALMING CABBAGE COOLER

vegan, sweet, paleo

While it may be surprising to find cabbage in a super smoothie, this recipe combines the light-tasting phytochemical-packed veggie with sweet fiber-rich apple and kiwi in an apple juice blend that packs a ton of nutrition into every sip. The smoothie helps to heal and maintain optimal functioning of the digestive system for greater health and improved immunity.

18 OUNCES

½ cup chopped red cabbage
1 Fuji apple, cored
1 kiwi
1 medium cucumber
1 cup organic apple juice (see Introduction)

1. In the 18-ounce NutriBullet cup, combine all ingredients.
2. Blend until all ingredients are thoroughly liquefied and combined, 30–60 seconds.
3. Consume immediately, or store with an airtight lid in the refrigerator for no more than 3–4 hours.

PER SERVING

CALORIES: 169	FAT: 1 G	PROTEIN: 1 G
SODIUM: 20 MG	FIBER: 4 G	
CARBOHYDRATES: 41 G		SUGAR: 24 G

TROPICAL TUMMY TREAT

vegan, sweet, paleo

Combining sweet and tangy fruits with cucumber and banana, this tropical treat's nutrient-dense content is already pretty remarkable. Add to the rich sources of vitamin C, biotin, and potassium the antioxidant- and phytochemical-rich aloe vera, and you've got a plethora of perfect nutrition that repairs and prevents tummy troubles of all kinds.

18 OUNCES

½ cup pineapple

1 medium cucumber

1 tangerine, peeled

1 banana, peeled and frozen

2 tablespoons aloe vera juice

1 cup organic apple juice (see Introduction)

1. In the 18-ounce NutriBullet cup, combine all ingredients.
2. Blend until all ingredients are thoroughly liquefied and combined, 30–60 seconds.
3. Consume immediately, or store with an airtight lid in the refrigerator for no more than 3–4 hours.

PER SERVING

CALORIES: 318	FAT: 1 G	PROTEIN: 3 G
SODIUM: 14 MG	FIBER: 7 G	
CARBOHYDRATES: 80 G		SUGAR: 58 G

GREEN YOUR DIGESTION

vegan, green, sweet, paleo

There's no question that fiber-rich greens are the perfect addition to any troubled-tummy diet, but the addition of apple, kiwi, aloe vera, and coconut oil add even more vitamins, minerals, antioxidants, and medium-chain fatty acids. They deliver the exact nutrition the gut needs to achieve a beneficial balance of bacteria, function optimally, and maintain a quality immune system.

18 OUNCES

¼ cup spinach
1 kale leaf
½ teaspoon seaweed
1 Fuji apple, cored
1 kiwi
2 tablespoons aloe vera juice
1 tablespoon coconut oil
1 cup organic apple juice (see Introduction)

1. In the 18-ounce NutriBullet cup, combine all ingredients.
2. Blend until all ingredients are thoroughly liquefied and combined, 30–60 seconds.
3. Consume immediately, or store with an airtight lid in the refrigerator for no more than 3–4 hours.

PER SERVING

CALORIES: 163	FAT: 1 G	PROTEIN: 3 G
SODIUM: 22 MG	FIBER: 3 G	
CARBOHYDRATES: 40 G		SUGAR: 24 G

CONSTIPATION CURE

vegan, green, sweet, paleo

Prunes have always been a go-to for constipation sufferers, and they take center stage in this delicious and nutritious super smoothie. It combines fiber-filled greens, apple, and banana, with a soothing addition of apple juice for a hydrating and refreshing snack or meal that will get things moving and help anyone achieve regularity . . . naturally!

18 OUNCES

2 kale leaves

1 cup prunes, pitted

½ Fuji apple, cored

1 banana, peeled and frozen

1 cup organic apple juice (see Introduction)

1. In the 18-ounce NutriBullet cup, combine all ingredients.
2. Blend until all ingredients are thoroughly liquefied and combined, 30–60 seconds.
3. Consume immediately, or store with an airtight lid in the refrigerator for no more than 3–4 hours.

PER SERVING

CALORIES: 627	FAT: 1 G	PROTEIN: 5 G
SODIUM: 15 MG	FIBER: 16 G	
CARBOHYDRATES: 164 G		SUGAR: 103 G

FUNNY TUMMY FIXER

vegan, green, sweet, paleo

Funny tummies can result from stress, spicy food, medications, or any of the conditions that disrupt functions performed by the digestive system. With fiber, protein, potassium, and antioxidants, this super smoothie provides the entire body with quality nutrition that supports all systems' functioning and delivers relief directly to the site of an upset stomach.

18 OUNCES

½ cup spinach
1 Fuji apple, cored
1 ounce cashews
1 banana, peeled and frozen
1 cup organic apple juice (see Introduction)

1. In the 18-ounce NutriBullet cup, combine all ingredients.
2. Blend until all ingredients are thoroughly liquefied and combined, 30–60 seconds.
3. Consume immediately, or store with an airtight lid in the refrigerator for no more than 3–4 hours.

PER SERVING

CALORIES: 454	FAT: 13 G	PROTEIN: 74 G
SODIUM: 26 MG	FIBER: 74 G	
CARBOHYDRATES: 84 G		SUGAR: 56 G

BERRIES FOR BETTER BELLIES

vegan, green, sweet, paleo

The anthocyanins and polyphenols contained within berries not only give these superfruits their beautiful hue but also act as powerful antioxidants that fight and protect against illness and disease. Combining these berries with fiber-rich spinach in a serving of apple juice provides a refreshing, rehydrating, and revitalizing blend of nutrition that supports the functions of the digestive system and helps maintain an optimal level of health.

18 OUNCES

½ cup blueberries

½ cup strawberries

½ cup blackberries

¼ cup spinach

1 cup organic apple juice (see Introduction)

1. In the 18-ounce NutriBullet cup, combine all ingredients.
2. Blend until all ingredients are thoroughly liquefied and combined, 30–60 seconds.
3. Consume immediately, or store with an airtight lid in the refrigerator for no more than 3–4 hours.

PER SERVING

CALORIES: 212	FAT: 1 G	PROTEIN: 2 G
SODIUM: 18 MG	FIBER: 8 G	
CARBOHYDRATES: 51 G		SUGAR: 38 G

SPICY SWEETNESS

vegan, sweet

Spiced up with ginger, this sweet blend of apple, banana, berries, and pineapple is the perfect snack or meal that provides the digestive system with valuable vibrant nutrition. With fiber, vitamins A, B_1, B_2, B_5, E, and C, potassium, magnesium, powerful phytochemicals, and ginger's unique enzymes and shagaol and gingerol oils, this super smoothie helps mend a troubled tummy.

18 OUNCES

1 Fuji apple, cored
½ banana, peeled and frozen
½ cup pineapple
¼ cup blueberries
¼" piece ginger, peeled
1 cup green tea, cooled

1. In the 18-ounce NutriBullet cup, combine all ingredients.
2. Blend until all ingredients are thoroughly liquefied and combined, 30–60 seconds.
3. Consume immediately, or store with an airtight lid in the refrigerator for no more than 3–4 hours.

PER SERVING

CALORIES: 192	FAT: 1 G	PROTEIN: 2 G
SODIUM: 2 MG	FIBER: 6 G	
CARBOHYDRATES: 50 G		SUGAR: 35 G

MELONS MEND ALL!

vegan, sweet, paleo

This light and refreshing super smoothie mixes two types of melons with sweet orange and spicy ginger. It makes for the perfect snack or meal that tastes great and provides the body with essential nutrients for optimal health and functioning. With a healthy dose of vitamin C, antioxidants, and ginger's shagaol and gingerol oils and enzymes, this recipe supports the digestive system and immune system.

18 OUNCES

½ cup cubed cantaloupe
½ cup cubed honeydew
1 orange, peeled
¼" piece ginger, peeled
1 cup purified water

1. In the 18-ounce NutriBullet cup, combine all ingredients.
2. Blend until all ingredients are thoroughly liquefied and combined, 30–60 seconds.
3. Consume immediately, or store with an airtight lid in the refrigerator for no more than 3–4 hours.

PER SERVING

CALORIES: 118	FAT: 0 G	PROTEIN: 2 G
SODIUM: 27 MG	FIBER: 5 G	
CARBOHYDRATES: 29 G		SUGAR: 25 G

CHAPTER 6

13 SMOOTHIES FOR BETTER HEART HEALTH

With a strong focus on heart health, these super smoothies optimize any health program or routine. These recipes emphasize fruits, vegetables, seeds, nuts, and additions that provide maximum antioxidants. They can help anyone achieve better heart health, cleaner blood, and maximum protection against illness and disease. Maximizing the nutrient availability of these super smoothies' superfoods, the NutriBullet blends and liquefies these foods so that nutrients that can be trapped in less broken-down forms of foods are delivered directly to the bloodstream and heart, and absorbed more easily throughout the digestive system. With delicious combinations of superfoods such as bananas and berries, spinach and kale, and nutty additions such as walnuts, cashews, flax seed, and nut milks, these super smoothies will help you succeed in your heart-health goals.

Simple, fast, and packed with amazing flavors, these smoothies can be snacks or meals, made morning, noon, or night. They'll optimize heart functioning while keeping you satisfied, full, and focused throughout the day or night. Whether your preference is sweet or savory, tropical or only slightly sweet, the recipes included in this chapter will fit your needs and help you achieve a greater sense of health, sip for sip and beat for beat!

HEALTHY BEETS FOR REGULAR BEATS

vegan, green, sweet, paleo

Beets' unique phytochemicals, betalains, combine with potassium-rich bananas and fiber-rich spinach to help support the health of the heart with essential minerals, cleansing fiber, and protective antioxidants.

18 OUNCES

1 red beet, greens removed, chopped

1 banana, peeled and frozen

½ cup spinach

1 cup organic apple juice (see Introduction)

1. In the 18-ounce NutriBullet cup, combine all ingredients.
2. Blend until all ingredients are thoroughly liquefied and combined, 30–60 seconds.
3. Consume immediately, or store with an airtight lid in the refrigerator for no more than 3–4 hours.

PER SERVING

CALORIES: 258	FAT: 1 G	PROTEIN: 3 G
SODIUM: 87 MG	FIBER: 6 G	
CARBOHYDRATES: 63 G		SUGAR: 44 G

NUTS ABOUT HEART HEALTH

vegan, green, sweet, paleo

Cashews and walnuts provide a healthy dose of protein and protective omegas to this sweet treat. The smoothie packs a punch of heart-healthy nutrition. The omega-3s, -6s, and -9s, beta-carotene, vitamins A and C, B vitamins, potassium, magnesium, and iron, along with a variety of vibrant antioxidants, help to keep the heart free of illness and disease.

18 OUNCES

1 ounce cashews

1 ounce walnuts

1 banana, peeled and frozen

1 peach, pitted

1 cup almond milk

1. In the 18-ounce NutriBullet cup, combine all ingredients.
2. Blend until all ingredients are thoroughly liquefied and combined, 30–60 seconds.
3. Consume immediately, or store with an airtight lid in the refrigerator for no more than 3–4 hours.

PER SERVING

CALORIES: 345	FAT: 19 G	PROTEIN: 7 G
SODIUM: 2 MG	FIBER: 7 G	
CARBOHYDRATES: 45 G		SUGAR: 27 G

GREENS FOR GREAT HEARTS

vegan, green, sweet, paleo

Free radicals are unstable atoms that seek to join with other atoms in the body and bloodstream, often damaging cells and triggering diseases, including cancer, in the process. Once free radical damage is done to cells, reversing the effects or preventing future damage is difficult. Through quality nutrition that provides protection and can help reverse free radical damage, a healthy body can stay healthy. Iron-rich greens combine with kiwi and avocado in this super smoothie for a slightly sweet, creamy treat that helps the blood remain clean of free radicals and the heart stay functioning as intended.

18 OUNCES

½ cup spinach

1 large kale leaf

½ teaspoon spirulina

1 small avocado, pitted and with skin removed

1 kiwi

1 cup organic apple juice (see Introduction)

1. In the 18-ounce NutriBullet cup, combine all ingredients.
2. Blend until all ingredients are thoroughly liquefied and combined, 30–60 seconds.
3. Consume immediately, or store with an airtight lid in the refrigerator for no more than 3–4 hours.

PER SERVING

CALORIES: 518	FAT: 30 G	PROTEIN: 8 G
SODIUM: 68 MG	FIBER: 18 G	
CARBOHYDRATES: 63 G		SUGAR: 25 G

CLEAN BEAN ANTIOXIDANT BLEND

vegan, green, sweet, paleo

Garbanzo beans take center stage in this nutritious blend as the main source of protein. The addition of extra protein from cashews, iron from spinach, and potassium from banana only improve the heart-health benefits that can be gained in each sip!

18 OUNCES

½ cup cooked garbanzo beans, rinsed and drained if canned

1 ounce raw cashews

½ cup spinach

1 banana, peeled and frozen

1 cup purified water

1. In the 18-ounce NutriBullet cup, combine all ingredients.
2. Blend until all ingredients are thoroughly liquefied and combined, 30–60 seconds.
3. Consume immediately, or store with an airtight lid in the refrigerator for no more than 3–4 hours.

PER SERVING

CALORIES: 627	FAT: 19 G	PROTEIN: 26 G
SODIUM: 40 MG	FIBER: 21 G	
CARBOHYDRATES: 96 G		SUGAR: 27 G

VERY VEGGIE

vegan, green, savory, paleo

This savory super smoothie makes for the perfect snack or meal any time of the day. Boosting heart health through their natural provisions of antioxidants, phytochemicals, enzymes, and oils, these nutrient-dense ingredients help improve and maintain overall health as well.

18 OUNCES

½ cup spinach

½ teaspoon spirulina

1 kale leaf

1 large tomato

¼ small red onion

1 clove garlic, peeled

1 cup purified water

1. In the 18-ounce NutriBullet cup, combine all ingredients.
2. Blend until all ingredients are thoroughly liquefied and combined, 30–60 seconds.
3. Consume immediately, or store with an airtight lid in the refrigerator for no more than 3–4 hours.

PER SERVING

CALORIES: 48	FAT: 0 G	PROTEIN: 2 G
SODIUM: 22 MG	FIBER: 3 G	
CARBOHYDRATES: 10 G		SUGAR: 6 G

GREAT GARLIC!

vegan, green, savory, paleo

While garlic isn't the most popular smoothie ingredient, it has enough nutrition that it should be. Providing blood-cleansing oils and enzymes, garlic combines with beta-carotene-packed carrots and vitamin K- and fiber-rich spinach and kale for a powerful antioxidant-loaded savory super smoothie. This delicious combo prevents illness and disease while supporting every aspect of the cardiovascular system for a strong body and healthy heart.

18 OUNCES

2 cloves garlic

½ cup spinach

1 kale leaf

1 large carrot, peeled and end removed, chopped

1 cup purified water

1. In the 18-ounce NutriBullet cup, combine all ingredients.
2. Blend until all ingredients are thoroughly liquefied and combined, 30–60 seconds.
3. Consume immediately, or store with an airtight lid in the refrigerator for no more than 3–4 hours.

PER SERVING

CALORIES: 42	FAT: 0 G	PROTEIN: 1 G
SODIUM: 63 MG	FIBER: 2 G	
CARBOHYDRATES: 9 G		SUGAR: 4 G

AWESOME AVOCADO

vegan, sweet, paleo

With healthy fats that not only help the heart to function but also reduce the harmful levels of cholesterol and triglycerides in the blood, avocados combine with delicious citrus fruits, blood-sugar-regulating aloe vera, and sweet apple juice for a sensational heart-healthy snack or meal.

18 OUNCES

1 small avocado, pitted and with skin removed

1 small red grapefruit, sectioned

1 tangerine, peeled

½ lemon

1 tablespoon aloe vera juice

1 cup organic apple juice (see Introduction)

1. In the 18-ounce NutriBullet cup, combine all ingredients.
2. Blend until all ingredients are thoroughly liquefied and combined, 30–60 seconds.
3. Consume immediately, or store with an airtight lid in the refrigerator for no more than 3–4 hours.

PER SERVING

CALORIES: 565	FAT: 30 G	PROTEIN: 7 G
SODIUM: 26 MG	FIBER: 18 G	
CARBOHYDRATES: 61 G		SUGAR: 50 G

OMEGA FIX WITH FLAX SEED

vegan, sweet, paleo

This collection of nutty and earthy ingredients plus sweet and spicy additions blends perfectly in the NutriBullet and provides an abundance of cell protection. The omega-3s and -6s, vitamins A, C, and E, antioxidants, calcium, and magnesium in this smoothie are powerful natural safeguards against free radical damage and illness.

18 OUNCES

1 ounce walnuts

1 tablespoon ground flax seed

1 large sweet potato, scrubbed thoroughly and skin intact

½ cup vanilla almond milk

1 teaspoon ground organic cinnamon

1. In the 18-ounce NutriBullet cup, combine all ingredients.
2. Blend until all ingredients are thoroughly liquefied and combined, 30–60 seconds.
3. Consume immediately, or store with an airtight lid in the refrigerator for no more than 3–4 hours.

PER SERVING

CALORIES: 348	FAT: 23 G	PROTEIN: 11 G
SODIUM: 19 MG	FIBER: 10 G	
CARBOHYDRATES: 39 G		SUGAR: 10 G

GREAT GREEN TOMATO

vegan, green, savory

Vibrant greens combine with juicy tomatoes and slightly spicy celery for a savory snack or meal that benefits the entire body. With antioxidants such as beta-carotene, minerals such as calcium and iron, and a variety of vitamins including A, Bs, and C, this nutritious combination of ingredients will put pep in your step and a smile on your face, all while keeping your body and especially your heart running right.

18 OUNCES

½ cup spinach
1 kale leaf
1 large tomato
1 celery stalk
½ cup green tea, cooled

1. In the 18-ounce NutriBullet cup, combine all ingredients.
2. Blend until all ingredients are thoroughly liquefied and combined, 30–60 seconds.
3. Consume immediately, or store with an airtight lid in the refrigerator for no more than 3–4 hours.

PER SERVING

CALORIES: 43	FAT: 0 G	PROTEIN: 2 G
SODIUM: 53 MG	FIBER: 3 G	
CARBOHYDRATES: 9 G		SUGAR: 6 G

SWEET CITRUS SPIN

vegan, green, sweet, paleo

Pineapple, kiwi, and pear combine with kale in smooth apple juice for a beautifully blended super smoothie that is light and refreshing but packed to the brim with nutrition. Vitamins A, B_3, B_5, and B_6, C, E, and K, iron, magnesium, fiber, and a plethora of antioxidants help to support the heart's functioning, keep the blood clean, and maintain a healthy beat for optimal blood flow!

18 OUNCES

1 kale leaf

1 Bartlett pear, cored

½ cup pineapple

1 kiwi

1 cup organic apple juice (see Introduction)

1. In the 18-ounce NutriBullet cup, combine all ingredients.
2. Blend until all ingredients are thoroughly liquefied and combined, 30–60 seconds.
3. Consume immediately, or store with an airtight lid in the refrigerator for no more than 3–4 hours.

PER SERVING

CALORIES: 202	FAT: 1 G	PROTEIN: 1 G
SODIUM: 15 MG	FIBER: 4 G	
CARBOHYDRATES: 50 G		SUGAR: 32 G

VANILLA ALMOND MILK TO BENEFIT ALL!

vegan, paleo

This easy-to-make super smoothie is one of the most delicious recipes for vanilla almond milk. It can be whipped up with additions such as bananas for a thicker consistency or blended just as the recipe instructs for a heart-healthy, all-natural almond milk that can be used in future smoothies, over cereal, or in just about any recipe that calls for milk.

18 OUNCES

1 cup raw almonds

2 cups purified water

Seeds scraped from 1 vanilla bean

1 tablespoon ground flax seed

1. In the 18-ounce NutriBullet cup, combine all ingredients.
2. Blend until all ingredients are thoroughly liquefied and combined, 30–60 seconds.
3. Consume immediately, or store with an airtight lid in the refrigerator for no more than 3–4 days.

PER SERVING

CALORIES: 546	FAT: 47 G	PROTEIN: 20 G
SODIUM: 1 MG	FIBER: 12 G	
CARBOHYDRATES: 21 G		SUGAR: 4 G

CASHEW MILK

vegan, paleo

This protein-packed cashew milk also provides heart-healthy omega-3s, -6s, and -9s for a perfectly blended taste sensation. You can use it in any smoothie recipe, substituting the cashew milk for a milk ingredient, or you can use it in other recipes or consume it on its own. Improving the systems' functioning throughout the body with natural provisions of vitamins, minerals, protein, healthy fats, and omegas, this recipe is a winner.

18 OUNCES

1 cup raw cashews

1 cup purified water

1 tablespoon ground flax seed

1. In the 18-ounce NutriBullet cup, combine all ingredients.
2. Blend until all ingredients are thoroughly liquefied and combined, 30–60 seconds.
3. Consume immediately, or store with an airtight lid in the refrigerator for no more than 3–4 days.

PER SERVING

CALORIES: 1,273	FAT: 100 G	PROTEIN: 43 G
SODIUM: 27 MG	FIBER: 10 G	
CARBOHYDRATES: 70 G		SUGAR: 13 G

KIWI-PEACH FOR BETTER BEATS

vegan, green, sweet, paleo

In this sweet smoothie, vitamins A, Bs, C, and E combine with iron, magnesium, and potassium as well as rich provisions of antioxidants from each ingredient. This super smoothie promotes a healthier heart while supporting all the body's organs and systems.

18 OUNCES

1 cup spinach

1 kale leaf

2 kiwis

1 peach, pitted

1 cup organic apple juice (see Introduction)

1. In the 18-ounce NutriBullet cup, combine all ingredients.
2. Blend until all ingredients are thoroughly liquefied and combined, 30–60 seconds.
3. Consume immediately, or store with an airtight lid in the refrigerator for no more than 3–4 hours.

PER SERVING

CALORIES: 271	FAT: 1 G	PROTEIN: 4 G
SODIUM: 41 MG	FIBER: 9 G	
CARBOHYDRATES: 66 G		SUGAR: 36 G

CHAPTER 7

13 SMOOTHIES FOR BETTER BLOOD SUGAR

Blood sugar levels can make or break a person's quality of life. Blood sugar fluctuates in response to the foods we eat and the physical demands we place on our bodies, causing variations in the energy we use to engage in activity, to focus, or to fall asleep. When blood sugar levels become erratic, the body suffers from anxiety, irregular heartbeats, energy spikes, mental fogginess, and/or "crashes." Serious illnesses and diseases can be adversely affected by blood sugar levels too, making this area of health a priority for anyone hoping to achieve optimal health.

The recipes in this chapter combine fruits, vegetables, and additions that are classified as "low glycemic index" foods (also known as "low GI" foods). These help achieve a stable blood sugar level and maintain that stabilized level without spikes and crashes that can result from the consumption of high GI foods. The NutriBullet can quickly extract the nutrients of these low GI superfoods and combine them into great-tasting snacks or meals for any time of the day to help provide your body and blood with natural resources for better blood sugar.

SWEET PEACH PREVENTION

sweet, paleo

The sweet peaches, almond milk, and heaping helping of omega-rich flax seed in this super smoothie won't wreak havoc on your blood sugar levels like so many other sweet treats. With fiber and antioxidants, along with a plethora of essential vitamins and minerals, this blood sugar–regulating combination is a sweet treat that keeps your levels perfectly balanced.

18 OUNCES

2 peaches, pitted
1 tablespoon ground flax seed
1½ cups vanilla almond milk

1. In the 18-ounce NutriBullet cup, combine all ingredients.
2. Blend until all ingredients are thoroughly liquefied and combined, 30–60 seconds.
3. Consume immediately, or store with an airtight lid in the refrigerator for no more than 3–4 hours.

PER SERVING

CALORIES: 211	FAT: 5 G	PROTEIN: 8 G
SODIUM: 49 MG	FIBER: 7 G	
CARBOHYDRATES: 37 G		SUGAR: 30 G

SPICY BLUE BLEND

vegan, sweet, paleo

Helping to cleanse the blood, regulate hormone production, and assist in insulin secretion, this delightful blend of ingredients provides powerful phytochemicals, antioxidants, amino acids, unique enzymes, and a variety of vitamins and minerals that help achieve better blood sugar levels.

18 OUNCES

1 cup blueberries

1 banana, peeled and frozen

1 tablespoon ground flax seed

¼" piece ginger, peeled

1 cup organic apple juice (see Introduction)

1. In the 18-ounce NutriBullet cup, combine all ingredients.
2. Blend until all ingredients are thoroughly liquefied and combined, 30–60 seconds.
3. Consume immediately, or store with an airtight lid in the refrigerator for no more than 3–4 hours.

PER SERVING

CALORIES: 338	FAT: 4 G	PROTEIN: 4 G
SODIUM: 13 MG	FIBER: 9 G	
CARBOHYDRATES: 78 G		SUGAR: 53 G

PEACH COBBLER

vegan, sweet

This peach cobbler perfection will actually help you achieve better blood sugar levels. With beta-carotene, potassium, and omegas, this blend of superfoods will help you achieve and maintain a better blood sugar content for sustained energy throughout the day.

18 OUNCES

1½ peaches, pitted

1 banana, peeled and frozen

½ cup rolled oats

1 ounce walnuts

1 teaspoon ground organic cinnamon

1 cup vanilla almond milk

1. In the 18-ounce NutriBullet cup, combine all ingredients.
2. Blend until all ingredients are thoroughly liquefied and combined, 30–60 seconds.
3. Consume immediately, or store with an airtight lid in the refrigerator for no more than 3–4 hours.

PER SERVING

CALORIES: 533	FAT: 22 G	PROTEIN: 13 G
SODIUM: 4 MG	FIBER: 14 G	
CARBOHYDRATES: 81 G		SUGAR: 34 G

AWESOME ALOE VERA

vegan, green, sweet, paleo

Although not to be taken along with other blood sugar regulators, aloe vera has been proven to lower blood sugar levels, support healthy hormone production, and assist in the enzymatic reactions that are involved with metabolism. Delicious and nutritious, this tropical treat is a naturally sweet snack or meal that will keep you full, focused, and energized for hours!

18 OUNCES

1 cup pineapple
1 banana, peeled and frozen
1 tablespoon aloe vera juice
½ teaspoon spirulina
1 tablespoon coconut oil
1 cup organic apple juice (see Introduction)

1. In the 18-ounce NutriBullet cup, combine all ingredients.
2. Blend until all ingredients are thoroughly liquefied and combined, 30–60 seconds.
3. Consume immediately, or store with an airtight lid in the refrigerator for no more than 3–4 hours.

PER SERVING

CALORIES: 302	FAT: 1 G	PROTEIN: 2 G
SODIUM: 13 MG	FIBER: 6 G	
CARBOHYDRATES: 77 G		SUGAR: 55 G

GARLICKY GREENS

vegan, green, savory, paleo

With a healthy dose of garlic, this savory super smoothie combines creamy avocado, vibrant greens, and liquid aloe vera to create a great snack or meal. Abundant antioxidants, vitamins, minerals, phytochemicals, and unique oils and enzymes make this smoothie one healthy way to achieve a stable blood sugar level that benefits the entire body.

18 OUNCES

½ cup spinach

2 kale leaves

½ teaspoon seaweed

1 medium avocado, pitted and with skin removed

2 garlic cloves

1 tablespoon aloe vera juice

1 cup purified water

1. In the 18-ounce NutriBullet cup, combine all ingredients.
2. Blend until all ingredients are thoroughly liquefied and combined, 30–60 seconds.
3. Consume immediately, or store with an airtight lid in the refrigerator for no more than 3–4 hours.

PER SERVING

CALORIES: 401	FAT: 30 G	PROTEIN: 9 G
SODIUM: 86 MG	FIBER: 16 G	
CARBOHYDRATES: 33 G		SUGAR: 1 G

BANANAS FOR BETTER BLOOD SUGAR

sweet, paleo

This spicy super smoothie is such a treat . . . and it's surprisingly nutritious. Packed with potassium, protein, and antioxidants, this blend of bananas and almond milk makes for the perfect sweet snack or dessert that won't spike your blood sugar and will help you achieve better health.

18 OUNCES

3 bananas, peeled and frozen

½ teaspoon ground organic cinnamon

¼ teaspoon ground cloves

1 cup almond milk

1. In the 18-ounce NutriBullet cup, combine all ingredients.
2. Blend until all ingredients are thoroughly liquefied and combined, 30–60 seconds.
3. Consume immediately, or store with an airtight lid in the refrigerator for no more than 3–4 hours.

PER SERVING

CALORIES: 320	FAT: 1 G	PROTEIN: 4 G
SODIUM: 5 MG	FIBER: 10 G	
CARBOHYDRATES: 82 G		SUGAR: 43 G

BERRY, BERRY MELONY

vegan, sweet, paleo

With refreshing cantaloupe and watermelon, this super smoothie adds fiber- and antioxidant-rich blueberries and ginger for an intense flavor combination that also improves health. This combination of low-glycemic foods is a tasty treat that helps every aspect of the body . . . including blood sugar levels, through the regulation of the very hormones that affect those levels.

18 OUNCES

½ cup cubed cantaloupe
½ cup cubed watermelon
1 cup blueberries
¼" piece ginger, peeled

1. In the 18-ounce NutriBullet cup, combine all ingredients.
2. Blend until all ingredients are thoroughly liquefied and combined, 30–60 seconds.
3. Consume immediately, or store with an airtight lid in the refrigerator for no more than 3–4 hours.

PER SERVING

CALORIES: 134	FAT: 1 G	PROTEIN: 2 G
SODIUM: 15 MG	FIBER: 5 G	
CARBOHYDRATES: 34 G		SUGAR: 26 G

RICH REGULATOR

sweet

Potassium-packed banana, beta-carotene-rich peach, blood-sugar-regulating oats, blood-cleansing flax seed, and protein-packed yogurt all combine in this super smoothie. It promotes a stable blood sugar level and provides protection and support to all of the body's systems and cells.

18 OUNCES

1 banana, peeled and frozen
1 peach, pitted
½ cup rolled oats
1 tablespoon ground flax seed
½ cup low-fat Greek yogurt
1 cup vanilla rice milk

1. In the 18-ounce NutriBullet cup, combine all ingredients.
2. Blend until all ingredients are thoroughly liquefied and combined, 30–60 seconds.
3. Consume immediately, or store with an airtight lid in the refrigerator for no more than 3–4 hours.

PER SERVING

CALORIES: 527	FAT: 11 G	PROTEIN: 22 G
SODIUM: 184 MG	FIBER: 13 G	
CARBOHYDRATES: 89 G		SUGAR: 43 G

SWEET AND SPICY GREENS

vegan, green, sweet, paleo

With fiber, antioxidants, and unique oils and enzymes, this combination of vibrant ingredients helps to cleanse the blood, regulate blood sugar levels, and improve digestion for an overall improvement of the body's functioning in every sweet and spicy sip.

18 OUNCES

2 kale leaves

½ teaspoon seaweed

½ cup blueberries

1 small Fuji apple, cored

¼" piece ginger, peeled

1 cup organic apple juice (see Introduction)

1. In the 18-ounce NutriBullet cup, combine all ingredients.
2. Blend until all ingredients are thoroughly liquefied and combined, 30–60 seconds.
3. Consume immediately, or store with an airtight lid in the refrigerator for no more than 3–4 hours.

PER SERVING

CALORIES: 219	FAT: 1 G	PROTEIN: 1 G
SODIUM: 13 MG	FIBER: 4 G	
CARBOHYDRATES: 55 G		SUGAR: 44 G

TEMPTING TOMATO TWIST

vegan, savory, paleo

The temptation of this tasty tomato super smoothie is one that's actually good to give in to. With beta-carotene, lycopene, flavonoids, and a number of vitamins, minerals, and naturally occurring polyphenols, this slightly spicy savory blend is a delicious and nutritious treat that helps to achieve and maintain better blood sugar levels for hours!

18 OUNCES

2 large tomatoes
¼ small red onion
1 garlic clove
2 tablespoons cilantro
½ cup purified water

1. In the 18-ounce NutriBullet cup, combine all ingredients.
2. Blend until all ingredients are thoroughly liquefied and combined, 30–60 seconds.
3. Consume immediately, or store with an airtight lid in the refrigerator for no more than 3–4 hours.

PER SERVING

CALORIES: 77	FAT: 1 G	PROTEIN: 4 G
SODIUM: 19 MG	FIBER: 5 G	
CARBOHYDRATES: 17 G		SUGAR: 10 G

NUTTY FOR BLOOD HEALTH

vegan, sweet, paleo

Bananas are the stars of this super smoothie, along with protein-packed nuts and omega-rich flax seed, which only intensify its nutritional goodness. This treat is packed with blood- and heart-healthy ingredients that improve the cardiovascular system's functioning and contribute to better blood sugar regulation.

18 OUNCES

2 bananas, peeled and frozen

1 ounce raw cashews

1 ounce walnuts

1 tablespoon ground flax seed

1 cup vanilla almond milk

1. In the 18-ounce NutriBullet cup, combine all ingredients.
2. Blend until all ingredients are thoroughly liquefied and combined, 30–60 seconds.
3. Consume immediately, or store with an airtight lid in the refrigerator for no more than 3–4 hours.

PER SERVING

CALORIES: 682	FAT: 37 G	PROTEIN: 19 G
SODIUM: 101 MG	FIBER: 12 G	
CARBOHYDRATES: 78 G		SUGAR: 38 G

PRICKLY PEAR

vegan, green, sweet, paleo

The prickliness of this refreshing smoothie is provided by the slightly spicy ginger. Adding a unique taste sensation to the spinach and pears, ginger improves the health benefits to the body, brain, and blood with its rich provisions of antioxidants, oils, and enzymes that cleanse the blood and support the healthy functioning of the entire cardiovascular system.

18 OUNCES

2 Bartlett pears, cored

½ cup spinach

¼" piece ginger, peeled

1 cup organic apple juice (see Introduction)

1. In the 18-ounce NutriBullet cup, combine all ingredients.
2. Blend until all ingredients are thoroughly liquefied and combined, 30–60 seconds.
3. Consume immediately, or store with an airtight lid in the refrigerator for no more than 3–4 hours.

PER SERVING

CALORIES: 310	FAT: 1 G	PROTEIN: 2 G
SODIUM: 25 MG	FIBER: 11 G	
CARBOHYDRATES: 80 G		SUGAR: 56 G

GINGER UP

vegan, sweet

With creamy banana and spicy ginger and a nutritious addition of aloe vera juice, this combination of ingredients makes for a tasty super smoothie with antioxidants, phytochemicals, fiber, and medium-chain fatty acids that support the healthy functioning of the heart and maintain healthy, stable blood sugar levels.

18 OUNCES

1 banana, peeled and frozen
½ cup blueberries
1 kiwi
¼" piece ginger, peeled
1 cup green tea, cooled
¼ cup aloe vera juice

1. In the 18-ounce NutriBullet cup, combine all ingredients.
2. Blend until all ingredients are thoroughly liquefied and combined, 30–60 seconds.
3. Consume immediately, or store with an airtight lid in the refrigerator for no more than 3–4 hours.

PER SERVING

CALORIES: 194	FAT: 1 G	PROTEIN: 3 G
SODIUM: 6 MG	FIBER: 7 G	
CARBOHYDRATES: 49 G		SUGAR: 22 G

CHAPTER 8

12 SMOOTHIES FOR ANTI-AGING

Whether you're trying to hold on to youth in its physical or its mental aspect, the superfoods in these super smoothies provide your body with the ultimate nutrition needed. Helping maintain skin elasticity, mental clarity, cognitive functioning, nerve functioning, and cardiovascular and digestive health, the citrus fruits, leafy greens, resveratrol-packed grapes, and enzymatic-reaction-supporting additions make for the perfect anti-aging smoothies.

Between the vitamins and minerals, antioxidants and phytochemicals, enzymes and healthy fats that these specialized blends of fruits, vegetables, and additions provide, it's easy to achieve and maintain good health. The essential nutrients needed to rejuvenate the body's systems and restore a youthfulness inside and out are found in the smoothies in this chapter. Helping to replenish the body's stores of vitamins and minerals, while providing protective antioxidants that fend off illness, disease, and oxidative stress, these super smoothies provide the perfect potions for anti-aging.

GREEN GRACE

vegan, green, sweet

Packed with antioxidants and restorative nutrients, this smoothie combines vibrant greens and sweet kiwis for a replenishing and refreshing snack or meal. It not only satisfies the appetite but also provides the body with quality nutrients that protect the cells and support every system's functioning. With plentiful vitamins, minerals, and phytochemicals, this blend of fruits and veggies is a delightful way to enjoy daily servings of proactive protection.

18 OUNCES

½ cup spinach

½ teaspoon spirulina

1 kale leaf

2 kiwis

1 cup green tea, cooled

1. In the 18-ounce NutriBullet cup, combine all ingredients.
2. Blend until all ingredients are thoroughly liquefied and combined, 30–60 seconds.
3. Consume immediately, or store with an airtight lid in the refrigerator for no more than 3–4 hours.

PER SERVING

CALORIES: 96	FAT: 1 G	PROTEIN: 2 G
SODIUM: 19 MG	FIBER: 5 G	
CARBOHYDRATES: 23 G		SUGAR: 0 G

PURPLE PURIFYING PINEAPPLE

vegan, sweet

Thanks to a sensual super smoothie that's as appealing to the eyes as it is to the taste buds, achieving optimal health and putting the brakes on the aging process has never been easier. Full of powerful protectant antioxidants, brain-fueling minerals, and rejuvenating nutrients that support the entire body's functioning, this smoothie's combination of fruits creates a purifying potion that makes you look, think, and feel beautifully young.

18 OUNCES

¼" piece of ginger, peeled
¼ cup blueberries
¼ cup blackberries
½ cup pineapple
1 cup green tea, cooled

1. In the 18-ounce NutriBullet cup, combine all ingredients.
2. Blend until all ingredients are thoroughly liquefied and combined, 30–60 seconds.
3. Consume immediately, or store with an airtight lid in the refrigerator for no more than 3–4 hours.

PER SERVING

CALORIES: 78	FAT: 0 G	PROTEIN: 1 G
SODIUM: 2 MG	FIBER: 4 G	
CARBOHYDRATES: 20 G		SUGAR: 14 G

RICH REVERSAL

vegan, sweet

Packing a punch with plentiful antioxidants and anti-inflammatory phytochemicals, this rich smoothie of delightfully delicious ingredients makes anti-aging efforts effortless. The benefits to the body spread from the digestive system to the heart, from the brain to the bones and muscles. Providing energy, stamina, and a host of anti-aging benefits, this Rich Reversal recipe is a winner in every area of health and beauty.

18 OUNCES

¼ cup strawberries
¼ cup blueberries
¼ cup red grapes
1 kiwi
1 cup green tea, cooled

1. In the 18-ounce NutriBullet cup, combine all ingredients.
2. Blend until all ingredients are thoroughly liquefied and combined, 30–60 seconds.
3. Consume immediately, or store with an airtight lid in the refrigerator for no more than 3–4 hours.

PER SERVING

CALORIES: 105	FAT: 1 G	PROTEIN: 2 G
SODIUM: 5 MG	FIBER: 5 G	
CARBOHYDRATES: 26 G		SUGAR: 11 G

BRAINS, BEAUTY, AND BRAWN

vegan, sweet, paleo

This yummy blend of fruits and spices promotes the health of the brain, heart, digestive system, skin, hair, nails, and eyes. With potassium, calcium, magnesium, antioxidants, and unique phytochemicals such as resveratrol, these super ingredients combine to create a spectacular super smoothie that promotes health on the inside and out.

18 OUNCES

2 bananas, peeled and frozen

½ cup frozen red grapes

1 tablespoon ground flax seed

1 teaspoon ground organic cinnamon

1 tablespoon aloe vera juice

1 cup unsweetened vanilla almond milk

1. In the 18-ounce NutriBullet cup, combine all ingredients.
2. Blend until all ingredients are thoroughly liquefied and combined, 30–60 seconds.
3. Consume immediately, or store with an airtight lid in the refrigerator for no more than 3–4 hours.

PER SERVING

CALORIES: 401	FAT: 7 G	PROTEIN: 10 G
SODIUM: 98 MG	FIBER: 11 G	
CARBOHYDRATES: 81 G		SUGAR: 47 G

TROPICAL TEMPTATION

vegan, sweet, paleo

The taste sensations of tropical flavors such as pineapple, banana, and kiwi boost the immune system with ample amounts of vitamin C. Aloe vera juice gives a nutritional boost. Packing in a plentiful array of antioxidants, vitamins, minerals, amino acids, and unique phytochemicals and enzymes, this super smoothie improves every area of the body and mind for a youthfulness you can see and feel.

18 OUNCES

1 cup pineapple
1 kiwi
1 small banana, peeled and frozen
1 tablespoon aloe vera juice
1 cup organic apple juice (see Introduction)

1. In the 18-ounce NutriBullet cup, combine all ingredients.
2. Blend until all ingredients are thoroughly liquefied and combined, 30–60 seconds.
3. Consume immediately, or store with an airtight lid in the refrigerator for no more than 3–4 hours.

PER SERVING

CALORIES: 333	FAT: 1 G	PROTEIN: 3 G
SODIUM: 16 MG	FIBER: 8 G	
CARBOHYDRATES: 84 G		SUGAR: 52 G

COGNITIVE CREATION

vegan, green, sweet, paleo

With brain-boosting omegas, this super smoothie provides the body and mind with cleansing phytochemicals and antioxidants that remove harmful toxins and fight the harmful effects of free radicals. Greens and carrots combine with nutty flavors of walnuts, flax seed, and almond milk that help promote optimal health throughout the entire body.

18 OUNCES

1 cup spinach

1 large carrot, peeled and end removed, chopped

½ banana, peeled and frozen

1 tablespoon ground flax seed

1 ounce walnuts

1 cup unsweetened almond milk

1. In the 18-ounce NutriBullet cup, combine all ingredients.
2. Blend until all ingredients are thoroughly liquefied and combined, 30–60 seconds.
3. Consume immediately, or store with an airtight lid in the refrigerator for no more than 3–4 hours.

PER SERVING

CALORIES: 272	FAT: 19 G	PROTEIN: 6 G
SODIUM: 75 MG	FIBER: 6 G	
CARBOHYDRATES: 25 G		SUGAR: 11 G

RESPIRATORY REFRESHER

sweet

With unique antioxidants called anthocyanidins found in berries, potassium and anti-inflammatory agents found in bananas, and the probiotic support of kefir, the respiratory system can function optimally and remain clean and clear of infection, inflammation, and harmful changes that can cause chronic conditions and illness.

18 OUNCES

½ cup blueberries

½ cup blackberries

1 medium banana, peeled and frozen

1 cup vanilla kefir

1. In the 18-ounce NutriBullet cup, combine all ingredients.
2. Blend until all ingredients are thoroughly liquefied and combined, 30–60 seconds.
3. Consume immediately, or store with an airtight lid in the refrigerator for no more than 3–4 hours.

PER SERVING

CALORIES: 178	FAT: 1 G	PROTEIN: 3 G
SODIUM: 3 MG	FIBER: 9 G	
CARBOHYDRATES: 45 G		SUGAR: 25 G

VEGGIES FOR VITALITY

vegan, green, savory

Deep green vitamin K-packed veggies combine with protein-rich cruciferous veggies for a healthy helping of quality nutrition. Antioxidants, which protect and support the body's natural immunity, abound in every sip. Safeguarding the cells and the body's systems from illness and disease, the powerful phytochemicals and fiber also help keep the body free of toxins and harmful oxidative free radicals.

18 OUNCES

½ cup spinach
2 kale leaves
¼ cup broccoli
¼ cup cauliflower
½ medium tomato
1 cup green tea, cooled

1. In the 18-ounce NutriBullet cup, combine all ingredients.
2. Blend until all ingredients are thoroughly liquefied and combined, 30–60 seconds.
3. Consume immediately, or store with an airtight lid in the refrigerator for no more than 3–4 hours.

PER SERVING

CALORIES: 29	FAT: 0 G	PROTEIN: 2 G
SODIUM: 30 MG	FIBER: 2 G	
CARBOHYDRATES: 5 G		SUGAR: 3 G

FIGHTING FIGS

vegan, sweet, paleo

With the power to fight off common colds, ferocious flus, and serious illness and disease, the phytochemicals and nutrients provided by this super smoothie's potent ingredients improve immunity, aid in proper digestion and regularity, and fight free radical damage on the inside and out, making it easy to stay healthy.

18 OUNCES

2 large figs, stems removed
1 Bartlett pear, cored
¼" piece ginger, peeled
1 cup organic apple juice (see Introduction)

1. In the 18-ounce NutriBullet cup, combine all ingredients.
2. Blend until all ingredients are thoroughly liquefied and combined, 30–60 seconds.
3. Consume immediately, or store with an airtight lid in the refrigerator for no more than 3–4 hours.

PER SERVING

CALORIES: 305	FAT: 1 G	PROTEIN: 2 G
SODIUM: 13 MG	FIBER: 9 G	
CARBOHYDRATES: 78 G		SUGAR: 61 G

MERRY MELONS

vegan, sweet, paleo

With a refreshing combination of sweet melons, spicy ginger, and coconut oil, the nutritional value of this super smoothie explodes with benefits that promote the health of the body and brain. Providing antioxidants, vitamins, minerals, unique enzymes, and medium-chain fatty acids, this super blend promotes the development of collagen and elastin, while fighting free radical damage that can wreak havoc on cells within the skin and throughout the body.

18 OUNCES

1 cup cubed cantaloupe
1 cup cubed honeydew
½" piece ginger, peeled
1 tablespoon coconut oil
½ cup purified water

1. In the 18-ounce NutriBullet cup, combine all ingredients.
2. Blend until all ingredients are thoroughly liquefied and combined, 30–60 seconds.
3. Consume immediately, or store with an airtight lid in the refrigerator for no more than 3–4 hours.

PER SERVING

CALORIES: 233	FAT: 14 G	PROTEIN: 2 G
SODIUM: 56 MG	FIBER: 3 G	
CARBOHYDRATES: 28 G		SUGAR: 26 G

GRAPES FOR GREATNESS

vegan, green, sweet

Resveratrol is one phytonutrient of grapes that takes center stage in this super smoothie. Acting as a powerful antioxidant that helps fight free radical damage in the eyes and skin while also protecting the health of the cells throughout the entire body, grapes pair perfectly with sweet pears, deep-green kale, and amino acid–rich aloe vera. Maintaining youthfulness never tasted so good.

18 OUNCES

1 cup red grapes, frozen
1 Bartlett pear, cored
1 large kale leaf
1 tablespoon aloe vera juice
1 cup green tea, cooled

1. In the 18-ounce NutriBullet cup, combine all ingredients.
2. Blend until all ingredients are thoroughly liquefied and combined, 30–60 seconds.
3. Consume immediately, or store with an airtight lid in the refrigerator for no more than 3–4 hours.

PER SERVING

CALORIES: 200	FAT: 0 G	PROTEIN: 2 G
SODIUM: 5 MG	FIBER: 7 G	
CARBOHYDRATES: 53 G		SUGAR: 40 G

KIWI-KALE CREATION

vegan, green, sweet

Sweet kiwis combine with kale and ginger for a delicious taste sensation that also promotes the healthy functioning of the entire body. Adding luscious aloe vera juice ups the ante of this nutritious delight and helps protect the health of the brain, improve digestion, and support the cardiovascular system.

18 OUNCES

2 kiwis

2 large kale leaves

¼" piece ginger, peeled

1 tablespoon aloe vera juice

1 cup organic apple juice (see Introduction)

1. In the 18-ounce NutriBullet cup, combine all ingredients.
2. Blend until all ingredients are thoroughly liquefied and combined, 30–60 seconds.
3. Consume immediately, or store with an airtight lid in the refrigerator for no more than 3–4 hours.

PER SERVING

CALORIES: 207	FAT: 1 G	PROTEIN: 2 G
SODIUM: 18 MG	FIBER: 6 G	
CARBOHYDRATES: 51 G		SUGAR: 24 G

CHAPTER 9

14 SMOOTHIES FOR GORGEOUS SKIN

To think that you can achieve youthful, blemish-free skin through a healthy diet lifestyle! The multi-billion-dollar-per-year skin care industry would crumble if people only realized how crucial and effective a healthy diet is in the pursuit of perfect skin. A super smoothie routine of the skin-benefiting ingredients packed into these recipes can help anyone achieve and maintain healthy, glowing skin. Choose from a variety of smoothies rich in the antioxidants, vitamins, nutrients, and enzymes that not only protect the skin against damage but also reverse the environment's unhealthy effects on the skin.

Incorporate these super smoothies as snacks or meals, once, twice, or three times daily. The NutriBullet will do a great job of extracting the nutrients' power contained within these fruits, vegetables, and additions. Using it, you can unharness the capabilities of natural nutrition to deliver the precise nutrients your skin needs to repair, restore, and replenish.

VITAMIN C FOR SUPPLE SKIN

sweet

Filled with vitamin C, this super smoothie delivers supple skin. It provides powerful antioxidants that can prevent and repair damage to the skin and body from oxidative stressors, which can wreak havoc on the skin's surface. This blend of rich fruits and restorative protein-rich yogurt makes for a delicious way to preserve your skin's beauty while also protecting your entire body's health.

18 OUNCES

1 medium orange, peeled
1 small tangerine, peeled
½ pink grapefruit, sectioned
½ cup low-fat Greek yogurt

1. In the 18-ounce NutriBullet cup, combine all ingredients.
2. Blend until all ingredients are thoroughly liquefied and combined, 30–60 seconds.
3. Consume immediately, or store with an airtight lid in the refrigerator for no more than 3–4 hours.

PER SERVING

CALORIES: 169	FAT: 4 G	PROTEIN: 6 G
SODIUM: 58 MG	FIBER: 3 G	
CARBOHYDRATES: 10 G		SUGAR: 29 G

SAVORY SKIN SAVER

vegan, green, savory, paleo

The unique blend of phytochemicals, nutrients, oils, and enzymes in this slightly savory smoothie benefits the skin immensely. In addition to improving the development of collagen and elastin, the aloe vera juice aids in preventing the sagging and fine lines that can occur in the skin. The vitamins, minerals, and antioxidants further protect, preserve, and support the skin's health.

18 OUNCES

1 medium avocado, pitted and with skin removed
1 celery stalk
1 cucumber
½ teaspoon spirulina
1 clove garlic
1 tablespoon aloe vera juice
1 cup purified water

1. In the 18-ounce NutriBullet cup, combine all ingredients.
2. Blend until all ingredients are thoroughly liquefied and combined, 30–60 seconds.
3. Consume immediately, or store with an airtight lid in the refrigerator for no more than 3–4 hours.

PER SERVING

CALORIES: 377	FAT: 30 G	PROTEIN: 6.5 G
SODIUM: 52 MG	FIBER: 16 G	
CARBOHYDRATES: 30 G		SUGAR: 7 G

MINTY RASPBERRY REVERSAL

sweet, paleo

The raspberries in this smoothie not only help support skin health with naturally occurring phytochemicals and powerful nutrients, but also protect skin from damage with potent antioxidants. Skin damage that occurs from toxins, sun exposure, or environmental issues can be improved with a healthy diet that includes daily doses of foods such as raspberries. Packed with vitamins, minerals, and antioxidants, this super smoothie is an excellent way to combat skin issues.

18 OUNCES

2 cups raspberries
1 cup vanilla almond milk
1 tablespoon chopped mint
½ cup purified water

1. In the 18-ounce NutriBullet cup, combine all ingredients.
2. Blend until all ingredients are thoroughly liquefied and combined, 30–60 seconds.
3. Consume immediately, or store with an airtight lid in the refrigerator for no more than 3–4 hours.

PER SERVING

CALORIES: 144	FAT: 2 G	PROTEIN: 4 G
SODIUM: 10 MG	FIBER: 16 G	
CARBOHYDRATES: 32 G		SUGAR: 12 G

POTENT PINEAPPLE PROTECTION

vegan, sweet, paleo

By promoting healthy collagen and elastin production, fending off free radical damage, reducing the appearance of fine lines and wrinkles, and reducing inflammation and unsightly redness and discoloration, the phytochemicals in this smoothie contribute to a clean, glowing complexion.

18 OUNCES

1 cup pineapple
1 cucumber
1 cup grapes
1 tablespoon aloe vera juice
1 tablespoon coconut oil
½ cup purified water

1. In the 18-ounce NutriBullet cup, combine all ingredients.
2. Blend until all ingredients are thoroughly liquefied and combined, 30–60 seconds.
3. Consume immediately, or store with an airtight lid in the refrigerator for no more than 3–4 hours.

PER SERVING

CALORIES: 351	FAT: 14 G	PROTEIN: 4 G
SODIUM: 11 MG	FIBER: 5 G	
CARBOHYDRATES: 60 G		SUGAR: 45 G

ACNE ALLEVIATOR

sweet

With healthy medium-chain fatty acids that regulate the oil production within the skin, along with a dose of vitamin C, B vitamins, potassium, magnesium, and antioxidants, this cleansing combination of fruits and additions provide the body and the skin with ingredients that help regulate hormones, control oil production, and minimize skin irritation. The result will be a better complexion with improved texture, less acne, and a more evenly toned appearance.

18 OUNCES

1 cup pineapple
1 banana, peeled and frozen
½ cup grapes
1 tablespoon aloe vera juice
1 tablespoon coconut oil
½ cup Greek yogurt

1. In the 18-ounce NutriBullet cup, combine all ingredients.
2. Blend until all ingredients are thoroughly liquefied and combined, 30–60 seconds.
3. Consume immediately, or store with an airtight lid in the refrigerator for no more than 3–4 hours.

PER SERVING

CALORIES: 433	FAT: 18 G	PROTEIN: 7 G
SODIUM: 61 MG	FIBER: 6 G	
CARBOHYDRATES: 68 G		SUGAR: 48 G

SWEET GREEN SKIN MACHINE

vegan, green, sweet, paleo

This delicious super smoothie's potent ingredients provide the body with antioxidants, vitamins, minerals, and unique enzymes that not only help support and protect the skin but encourage new, healthy collagen and elastin production for improved health and beauty for years to come.

18 OUNCES

½ cup spinach
½ teaspoon seaweed
1 cup pineapple
½ cup green tea, cooled
1 tablespoon aloe vera juice
1 tablespoon coconut oil

1. In the 18-ounce NutriBullet cup, combine all ingredients.
2. Blend until all ingredients are thoroughly liquefied and combined, 30–60 seconds.
3. Consume immediately, or store with an airtight lid in the refrigerator for no more than 3–4 hours.

PER SERVING

CALORIES: 205	FAT: 14 G	PROTEIN: 1 G
SODIUM: 15 MG	FIBER: 3 G	
CARBOHYDRATES: 22 G		SUGAR: 16 G

SUN-DAMAGE SOOTHER

sweet

Even though the consensus about sun exposure is that it can be extremely harmful to the skin, the sun's rays can be difficult to avoid. This super smoothie is a delicious way to soothe the skin after sun exposure. Beta-carotene-rich sweet potato protects the skin with powerful antioxidants. Both it and aloe vera have unique enzymes and oils that prevent cancerous changes within the skin's cells. And protein-rich yogurt supports the skin's health with the added benefits of minerals like calcium and potassium, for maximum nutrition that helps protect and maintain the health and appearance of the skin.

18 OUNCES

1 sweet potato, cleaned thoroughly, skin intact
1 teaspoon ground cardamom
3 tablespoons aloe vera juice
1 cup Greek yogurt

1. In the 18-ounce NutriBullet cup, combine all ingredients.
2. Blend until all ingredients are thoroughly liquefied and combined, 30–60 seconds.
3. Consume immediately, or store with an airtight lid in the refrigerator for no more than 3–4 hours.

PER SERVING

CALORIES: 267	FAT: 8 G	PROTEIN: 11 G
SODIUM: 184 MG	FIBER: 4 G	
CARBOHYDRATES: 38 G		SUGAR: 17 G

BERRY, MERRY SKIN

sweet

This simple combination of phytochemical-rich fruits and protein-packed yogurt makes for a super smoothie that is delicious to sip and beyond beneficial for your skin. Included in this delightful smoothie are vitamins, minerals, phytochemicals, and enzymes that help protect the skin from free radical damage and replenish the skin's multiple layers with new healthy cells.

18 OUNCES

½ cup strawberries
½ cup blueberries
1 banana, peeled and frozen
½ cup low-fat Greek yogurt
2 tablespoons aloe vera juice

1. In the 18-ounce NutriBullet cup, combine all ingredients.
2. Blend until all ingredients are thoroughly liquefied and combined, 30–60 seconds.
3. Consume immediately, or store with an airtight lid in the refrigerator for no more than 3–4 hours.

PER SERVING

CALORIES: 244	FAT: 5 G	PROTEIN: 7 G
SODIUM: 59 MG	FIBER: 6 G	
CARBOHYDRATES: 48 G		SUGAR: 31 G

CUCUMBERS FOR COOLER COMPLEXION

vegan, sweet

With hydrating ingredients that provide their own unique phytochemicals, this super smoothie contributes to the skin's health in a number of ways: protecting against dangerous changes within the skin and its cells, improving the production of elastin and collagen, and supporting the skin's health and appearance through hormonal balance. This super smoothie's ingredients build a cool complexion with every sip.

18 OUNCES

2 large cucumbers
2 tablespoons chopped mint
1 tablespoon aloe vera juice
¼" piece ginger, peeled
1 cup green tea, cooled

1. In the 18-ounce NutriBullet cup, combine all ingredients.
2. Blend until all ingredients are thoroughly liquefied and combined, 30–60 seconds.
3. Consume immediately, or store with an airtight lid in the refrigerator for no more than 3–4 hours.

PER SERVING

CALORIES: 99	FAT: 1 G	PROTEIN: 5 G
SODIUM: 23 MG	FIBER: 4 G	
CARBOHYDRATES: 23 G		SUGAR: 10 G

Aloe's Anti-Aging Benefits

With skin-rejuvenating polyphenols that promote the healthy regeneration of skin cells, aloe vera not only helps restore collagen and elastin for youthful appearance within the skin's surface but also provides essential anti-aging antioxidants that protect against free radical damage and serious disease and illness.

CLEAR COMPLEXION COCKTAIL

vegan, savory, paleo

Every single sip of this savory super smoothie contains nutrients and phytochemicals that provide benefits throughout the entire body! This delicious and nutritious blend of powerful ingredients helps maintain a clear complexion, and gives the skin a more youthful glow that can only be achieved with nature's own medicine: good nutrition!

18 OUNCES

1 small tomato

½ medium cucumber

1 celery stalk

1 tablespoon chopped red onion

1 clove garlic

1 tablespoon aloe vera juice

1 tablespoon coconut oil

¼ cup purified water

1. In the 18-ounce NutriBullet cup, combine all ingredients.
2. Blend until all ingredients are thoroughly liquefied and combined, 30–60 seconds.
3. Consume immediately, or store with an airtight lid in the refrigerator for no more than 3–4 hours.

PER SERVING

CALORIES: 173	FAT: 14 G	PROTEIN: 2 G
SODIUM: 40 MG	FIBER: 3 G	
CARBOHYDRATES: 12 G		SUGAR: 6 G

A Small Dose of Spiciness for a Load of Prevention

With its abundance of antioxidants, the slightly spicy red onion adds a potent amount of powerhouse nutrition to any super smoothie. This allicin-rich vegetable packs a ton of antioxidants and anti-inflammatory compounds into every sip of savory smoothies while adding the kick of a little extra spice.

PRICKLY PEAR FOR PERFECTION

vegan, sweet

It's easy to see why this super smoothie can help achieve skin perfection. With light-tasting ingredients that hydrate the body, packing a punch of protective antioxidants while promoting the skin's regeneration of essential cells, this delicious and nutritious mix is the perfect blend for perfect skin.

18 OUNCES

1 large Bartlett pear, cored
1 medium cucumber
¼" piece ginger, peeled
1 tablespoon aloe vera juice
¾ cup green tea, cooled

1. In the 18-ounce NutriBullet cup, combine all ingredients.
2. Blend until all ingredients are thoroughly liquefied and combined, 30–60 seconds.
3. Consume immediately, or store with an airtight lid in the refrigerator for no more than 3–4 hours.

PER SERVING

CALORIES: 310	FAT: 1 G	PROTEIN: 2 G
SODIUM: 25 MG	FIBER: 7 G	
CARBOHYDRATES: 80 G		SUGAR: 56 G

DE-LIGHT-FULLY DELICIOUS!

sweet

This sweet, creamy super smoothie is a light and satisfying way to sip yourself to spectacular skin health! Brimming with vibrant and valuable nutrients and powerful phytochemicals that help prevent cellular distress within the skin, this tropical treat is a wonderful way to reverse and prevent skin damage.

18 OUNCES

1 cup pineapple

1 banana, peeled and frozen

1 cup nonfat Greek yogurt

½ teaspoon ground organic cinnamon

1. In the 18-ounce NutriBullet cup, combine all ingredients.
2. Blend until all ingredients are thoroughly liquefied and combined, 30–60 seconds.
3. Consume immediately, or store with an airtight lid in the refrigerator for no more than 3–4 hours.

PER SERVING

CALORIES: 339	FAT: 9 G	PROTEIN: 11 G
SODIUM: 116 MG	FIBER: 6 G	
CARBOHYDRATES: 61 G		SUGAR: 42 G

GREEN GREATNESS

vegan, green, sweet, paleo

The vibrant color and taste of this smoothie reveal the vitality of the superfoods that created it. With each powerful superfood contributing to its rich stores of vitamins A, C, E, and K, minerals including biotin, iron, calcium, and magnesium, and powerful antioxidants and anti-inflammatory agents, this super smoothie generates improved cell functioning and antioxidative protection within the skin's every cell.

18 OUNCES

½ cup spinach
1 kale leaf
2 kiwis
1 small cucumber
1 tablespoon aloe vera juice
1 cup purified water

1. In the 18-ounce NutriBullet cup, combine all ingredients.
2. Blend until all ingredients are thoroughly liquefied and combined, 30–60 seconds.
3. Consume immediately, or store with an airtight lid in the refrigerator for no more than 3–4 hours.

PER SERVING

CALORIES: 141	FAT: 1 G	PROTEIN: 4 G
SODIUM: 25 MG	FIBER: 7 G	
CARBOHYDRATES: 34 G		SUGAR: 5 G

PEACHY PERFECTION

sweet, paleo

Bright beta-carotene and its antioxidant effects that benefits the body, brain, and skin combine with omega-rich flax seed, enzymes and oils from the spices and aloe, and protein-packed yogurt for a sweet snack or meal. This super smoothie is nutrient-dense enough to optimize overall health, but almost tastes too delicious to be this nutritious.

18 OUNCES

2 peaches, pitted

1 tablespoon ground flax seed

½ teaspoon ground organic cinnamon

1 tablespoon aloe vera juice

1 cup low-fat vanilla almond milk

½ cup purified water

1. In the 18-ounce NutriBullet cup, combine all ingredients.
2. Blend until all ingredients are thoroughly liquefied and combined, 30–60 seconds.
3. Consume immediately, or store with an airtight lid in the refrigerator for no more than 3–4 hours.

PER SERVING

CALORIES: 360	FAT: 6 G	PROTEIN: 16 G
SODIUM: 161 MG	FIBER: 7 G	
CARBOHYDRATES: 65 G		SUGAR: 59 G

CHAPTER 10

13 SMOOTHIES THAT REDUCE INFLAMMATION

Inflammation is not only a physical change that takes place in the body; it can also be a painful symptom of an underlying health issue. You can see inflammation wherever you sustain an injury in which swelling appears. Inflammation at the site of an injury is the body's way of calling much-needed blood cells and natural purging agents to the scene to restore health to surrounding tissues and protect those tissues from microbes, bacteria, etc. that could cause infection. Inflammation can also occur on a cellular level, as a result of oxidative stress, which can lead to harmful cellular changes that create chronic disease. Arthritis is a form of inflammation, wreaking havoc on the joints and causing pain, swelling, and minimized mobility.

Luckily, through a diet that focuses on improving the immune system while maximizing cellular health and promoting the lubrication and health of the joints, you can dramatically reduce the incidence of inflammation. Here's where your NutriBullet comes in, creating super smoothies that will support the cells and systems of your entire body while helping to make inflammation (and all of its effects) a thing of the past!

INFLAMMATION IMMUNITY

sweet

Oh, the taste of cherries! They're the stars of this smoothie, providing a plethora of powerful phytochemicals that act as anti-inflammatory agents and antioxidants, helping to reduce inflammation throughout the body. Add to them a healthy helping of calcium- and protein-rich yogurt and omega-rich flax seed and you've got a sweet prescription for preventing inflammation.

18 OUNCES

1 cup cherries, pitted
1 cup nonfat Greek yogurt
1 tablespoon ground flax seed
½ cup purified water

1. In the 18-ounce NutriBullet cup, combine all ingredients.
2. Blend until all ingredients are thoroughly liquefied and combined, 30–60 seconds.
3. Consume immediately, or store with an airtight lid in the refrigerator for no more than 3–4 hours.

PER SERVING

CALORIES: 227	FAT: 3 G	PROTEIN: 12 G
SODIUM: 132 MG	FIBER: 6 G	
CARBOHYDRATES: 44 G		SUGAR: 37 G

Amazing Antioxidants

Not only do these free-radical-fighting phytochemicals combat debilitating damage to the healthy cells throughout the body's intricate network of systems and functions; they also promote and protect the health of cells by combating toxic interference and oxidative stress, adding to their immunity-building powers that help keep serious illness at bay.

FEND OFF INFLAMMATORY DISEASE

vegan, green, sweet

With chronic inflammation, the body begins to develop other chronic conditions such as arthritis, buildup and hardening of tissues, and even unhealthy cellular changes. With potent vitamins, minerals, and phytochemicals that act as powerful anti-inflammatory antioxidants from delicious ingredients like kale, kiwi, blueberries, ginger, and aloe, this smoothie pleases the taste buds while preventing inflammation and repairing its effects.

18 OUNCES

1 kale leaf

1 kiwi

½ cup blueberries

¼" piece ginger, peeled

1 tablespoon aloe vera juice

½ cup green tea, cooled

1. In the 18-ounce NutriBullet cup, combine all ingredients.
2. Blend until all ingredients are thoroughly liquefied and combined, 30–60 seconds.
3. Consume immediately, or store with an airtight lid in the refrigerator for no more than 3–4 hours.

PER SERVING

CALORIES: 89	FAT: 1 G	PROTEIN: 1 G
SODIUM: 5 MG	FIBER: 4 G	
CARBOHYDRATES: 22 G		SUGAR: 7 G

AWAY WITH ARTHRITIS!

vegan, sweet

Arthritis can be a painful and debilitating disease that flares at one site or spreads throughout the body. With naturally nutrient-dense foods like betalain-rich beets and fiber-rich bananas, plus kiwi's vitamin C and aloe's vitamin E, this super smoothie offers powerful protection against arthritis.

18 OUNCES

1 red beet, greens removed, chopped

½ banana, peeled and frozen

1 kiwi

1 tablespoon aloe vera juice

½ cup green tea, cooled

1. In the 18-ounce NutriBullet cup, combine all ingredients.
2. Blend until all ingredients are thoroughly liquefied and combined, 30–60 seconds.
3. Consume immediately, or store with an airtight lid in the refrigerator for no more than 3–4 hours.

PER SERVING

CALORIES: 134	FAT: 1 G	PROTEIN: 3 G
SODIUM: 68 MG	FIBER: 6 G	
CARBOHYDRATES: 33 G		SUGAR: 13 G

FLEXIBILITY FOUND!

sweet

Bananas, walnuts, flax seed, and Greek yogurt are blended in this super smoothie. The result is a snack or meal that not only satisfies hunger but promotes the natural lubrication of the joints, prevents inflammatory damage caused to cells, and assists in the regeneration of tissue that may have been degraded by past or present inflammation. With all of these benefits targeting your body's stiffest points, you'll appreciate newfound flexibility and comfort.

18 OUNCES

2 bananas, peeled and frozen
1 ounce walnuts
1 tablespoon ground flax seed
1 tablespoon aloe vera juice
1 cup nonfat Greek yogurt
¼ cup purified water

1. In the 18-ounce NutriBullet cup, combine all ingredients.
2. Blend until all ingredients are thoroughly liquefied and combined, 30–60 seconds.
3. Consume immediately, or store with an airtight lid in the refrigerator for no more than 3–4 hours.

PER SERVING

CALORIES: 428	FAT: 22 G	PROTEIN: 9 G
SODIUM: 3 MG	FIBER: 10 G	
CARBOHYDRATES: 60 G		SUGAR: 30 G

FORGO INFLAMMATION WITH FRUITINESS

sweet

Beautiful berries, creamy yogurt, wholesome oats, and nutty flax seed make up this delicious super smoothie. Deep red and blue anthocyanin pigments and rich polyphenols act as natural anti-inflammatory antioxidants and combine with inflammation-calming calcium, vitamin E, and B vitamins for a delicious way to minimize inflammation.

18 OUNCES

½ cup strawberries
½ cup blueberries
¼ cup raw rolled oats
1 tablespoon ground flax seed
½ cup nonfat Greek yogurt

1. In the 18-ounce NutriBullet cup, combine all ingredients.
2. Blend until all ingredients are thoroughly liquefied and combined, 30–60 seconds.
3. Consume immediately, or store with an airtight lid in the refrigerator for no more than 3–4 hours.

PER SERVING

CALORIES: 225	FAT: 5 G	PROTEIN: 10 G
SODIUM: 68 MG	FIBER: 8 G	
CARBOHYDRATES: 41 G		SUGAR: 19 G

Anti-Inflammatory Nutrition

With plentiful antioxidants and a number of powerhouse anti-inflammatory phytochemicals, the superfoods you love to add to your favorite smoothies can help curb chronic illness, protect cells against degradation, and safeguard the immune system against illness and disease . . . all with the flavors of nature's sweetest and most savory treats!

DELICIOUS DEFENSE

vegan, green, savory, paleo

This savory smoothie blends together a variety of vibrant vegetables that hydrate the body, prevent inflammation, reverse damage from inflammation and promote joint health. With lycopene-laden tomatoes, calcium- and iron-rich spinach, and antioxidant-packed onion, garlic, and spices, this unique combination of cool ingredients will spice up your life and soothe your arthritis.

18 OUNCES

½ cup spinach
1 small tomato
2 tablespoons chopped red onion
1 garlic clove
½ teaspoon ground turmeric
1 tablespoon aloe vera juice
½ cup purified water

1. In the 18-ounce NutriBullet cup, combine all ingredients.
2. Blend until all ingredients are thoroughly liquefied and combined, 30–60 seconds.
3. Consume immediately, or store with an airtight lid in the refrigerator for no more than 3–4 hours.

PER SERVING

CALORIES: 36	FAT: 0 G	PROTEIN: 2 G
SODIUM: 18 MG	FIBER: 2 G	
CARBOHYDRATES: 7 G		SUGAR: 3 G

Berries Doing Double Duty

With unique phytochemicals such as anthocyanins and anthocyanidins that give berries their vibrant hues, all varieties of this fruit provide the body with double doses of powerful immune system protection. Those phytochemicals act as antioxidants that protect against cell damage, while their rich content of vitamin C adds additional support to the immune system and the cells.

GREAT GREEN GRACEFULNESS

vegan, green, sweet, paleo

The graceful splendor of this super smoothie is not limited to its beautiful hue or its delicious taste. It also includes powerful antioxidants that combat cell damage, vitamins A, C, E, and K, and minerals such as iron, calcium, potassium, and magnesium for improved immunity and system functioning.

18 OUNCES

½ cup spinach

½ Bartlett pear, cored

½ banana, peeled and frozen

½ cup organic apple juice (see Introduction)

1. In the 18-ounce NutriBullet cup, combine all ingredients.
2. Blend until all ingredients are thoroughly liquefied and combined, 30–60 seconds.
3. Consume immediately, or store with an airtight lid in the refrigerator for no more than 3–4 hours.

PER SERVING

CALORIES: 161	FAT: 1 G	PROTEIN: 2 G
SODIUM: 18 MG	FIBER: 5 G	
CARBOHYDRATES: 41 G		SUGAR: 27 G

SWEET AND SIMPLE CELL PROTECTION

sweet, paleo

The antioxidants that abound in every ounce of this smoothie help protect cells' health in every way. By promoting the regeneration of healthy cells, protecting existing cells from oxidative stress and inflammatory damage, and preventing inflammation from causing future stress and damage to cells and systems, the anti-inflammatory compounds and antioxidants of these potent ingredients work together to reduce and prevent pain.

18 OUNCES

1 cup blueberries

1 banana, peeled and frozen

1 cup vanilla almond milk

1 tablespoon aloe vera juice

1. In the 18-ounce NutriBullet cup, combine all ingredients.
2. Blend until all ingredients are thoroughly liquefied and combined, 30–60 seconds.
3. Consume immediately, or store with an airtight lid in the refrigerator for no more than 3–4 hours.

PER SERVING

CALORIES: 237	FAT: 1 G	PROTEIN: 7 G
SODIUM: 69 MG	FIBER: 7 G	
CARBOHYDRATES: 57 G		SUGAR: 38 G

AWESOME OXIDATIVE REVERSAL

vegan, green, sweet, paleo

Oxidative damage is the inflammatory effect on cells that can create a chronic condition or lead to a serious illness. With each ingredient providing its own unique phytochemicals that act as powerful antioxidants, this smoothie is a protective potion that can safeguard against oxidative stress and damage, and promote cell health for years.

18 OUNCES

1 cup cherries, pitted
¼ cup spinach
1 small Fuji apple, cored
1 cup purified water

1. In the 18-ounce NutriBullet cup, combine all ingredients.
2. Blend until all ingredients are thoroughly liquefied and combined, 30–60 seconds.
3. Consume immediately, or store with an airtight lid in the refrigerator for no more than 3–4 hours.

PER SERVING

CALORIES: 162	FAT: 1 G	PROTEIN: 2 G
SODIUM: 6 MG	FIBER: 5 G	
CARBOHYDRATES: 42 G		SUGAR: 33 G

Apples Abound with Benefits

Picking the perfect apple for your super smoothie makes for a delicious and nutritious step in the right direction for overall health. With unique phytochemicals and antioxidants, apples provide the body with vitamin C, fiber, and quercetin for improved digestion, maximum detoxification, and pumped-up protection against illness and disease.

YOUTHFUL YOGURT BLISS

sweet

A slightly sweet super smoothie of antioxidant-abundant strawberries, protein-packed yogurt, and enzyme-rich ginger not only provides the body with nutrition that promotes anti-inflammatory protection, but also encourages optimal joint, nerve, and systemic health that improves functioning.

18 OUNCES

1 cup strawberries
½ cup nonfat Greek yogurt
¼" piece ginger, peeled
¼ cup aloe vera juice

1. In the 18-ounce NutriBullet cup, combine all ingredients.
2. Blend until all ingredients are thoroughly liquefied and combined, 30–60 seconds.
3. Consume immediately, or store with an airtight lid in the refrigerator for no more than 3–4 hours.

PER SERVING

CALORIES: 94	FAT: 1 G	PROTEIN: 5 G
SODIUM: 67 MG	FIBER: 3 G	
CARBOHYDRATES: 19 G		SUGAR: 15 G

SWEET SOOTHING CITRUS

vegan, sweet, paleo

Vitamin C does double duty in this super-sweet smoothie for a plethora of benefits that promote immunity, optimize health, and improve conditions and symptoms related to inflammation. Vitamin C provides powerful antioxidants to protect the body against disease. This blend of soothing fruits and ginger also attacks inflammation with powerful anti-inflammatory phytochemicals.

18 OUNCES

1 orange, peeled
½ cup strawberries
½ cup pineapple
1 kiwi
¼" piece ginger, peeled
1 cup purified water

1. In the 18-ounce NutriBullet cup, combine all ingredients.
2. Blend until all ingredients are thoroughly liquefied and combined, 30–60 seconds.
3. Consume immediately, or store with an airtight lid in the refrigerator for no more than 3–4 hours.

PER SERVING

CALORIES: 172	FAT: 1 G	PROTEIN: 3 G
SODIUM: 5 MG	FIBER: 8 G	
CARBOHYDRATES: 43 G		SUGAR: 24 G

Bromelain for Bruises

A little-known fact about pineapple is that it contains a unique phytochemical called bromelain that has been proven to reduce the appearance and duration of bruising. By improving blood flow, removing damaged blood vessels, and clearing the bloodstream of toxins, this antioxidant helps to relieve bruises naturally while providing the body with cleansing and detoxifying benefits.

ACHES, BE GONE!

sweet

With fruits that combine to create a sweet smoothie packed with antioxidants, anti-inflammatory compounds, vitamin C, B vitamins, bromelain, and protein, this is a simple, powerful protective potion.

18 OUNCES

½ cup cherries, pitted
½ cup pineapple
½ banana, peeled and frozen
½ cup low-fat Greek yogurt

1. In the 18-ounce NutriBullet cup, combine all ingredients.
2. Blend until all ingredients are thoroughly liquefied and combined, 30–60 seconds.
3. Consume immediately, or store with an airtight lid in the refrigerator for no more than 3–4 hours.

PER SERVING

CALORIES: 216	FAT: 4 G	PROTEIN: 6 G
SODIUM: 57 MG	FIBER: 4 G	
CARBOHYDRATES: 42 G		SUGAR: 31 G

TROPICAL INFLAMMATION TAMER

sweet

Deliciously sweet tropical fruits like pineapple, banana, and kiwi take center stage in this inflammation-taming smoothie that also includes yogurt and aloe vera. A taste sensation, this antioxidant-rich blend of superfoods makes for an anti-inflammatory blend you won't mind sipping as a snack, meal, or dessert.

18 OUNCES

½ cup pineapple
1 kiwi
½ banana, peeled and frozen
2 tablespoons aloe vera juice
½ cup nonfat Greek yogurt

1. In the 18-ounce NutriBullet cup, combine all ingredients.
2. Blend until all ingredients are thoroughly liquefied and combined, 30–60 seconds.
3. Consume immediately, or store with an airtight lid in the refrigerator for no more than 3–4 hours.

PER SERVING

CALORIES: 188	FAT: 1 G	PROTEIN: 6 G
SODIUM: 71 MG	FIBER: 5 G	
CARBOHYDRATES: 44 G		SUGAR: 24 G

Yogurt for Yummy Benefits

Yogurt adds plenty of quality nutrients to any super smoothie: probiotics, calcium, B vitamins, protein, and zinc. Helping to cleanse the colon, increase the bacterial benefits in the gut, improve immunity, and support the brain and bodily systems' functioning, yogurt is an addition worthy of the superfood label.

CHAPTER 11

13 SMOOTHIES THAT ENERGIZE

High energy levels that last throughout the day offer improvements to your body, mind, and quality of life. Long-lasting energy can transform your days from tedious hours of ebbs and flows of vitality to productive, enjoyable hours of increased focus, improved mental clarity, and a level of physical performance you never dreamed possible. Many people have grown accustomed to regular energy highs and lows that require caffeine, sugar, or constant snacking. With a simple schedule of regular meals and snacks that provide the body with proper nutrition, though, anyone can improve his or her energy levels quickly and naturally.

The recipes in this chapter illustrate how you can use your NutriBullet to create delicious and nutritious smoothies that improve your energy levels and let you enjoy that newfound energy throughout the entire day. Adding just one or two super smoothies per day, you can transform your nutrient-deficient diet to one of long-lasting, high-energy nutrition that not only helps you stay fit, focused, and alert but also optimizes the health of every cell in your body.

CARROT-BROCCOLI BLAST-OFF

vegan, savory

With the right ingredients, you can create the perfect super smoothie that empowers your body and energizes your day. This clean carbohydrate-fueled blend of iron-rich greens, protein-packed broccoli, vitamins A, C, E, and K, and minerals including calcium, magnesium, and potassium can help you perform at your best with energy that lasts.

18 OUNCES

½ cup broccoli florets

2 carrots, peeled and greens removed, chopped

¼ cup spinach

1 cup purified water

1. In the 18-ounce NutriBullet cup, combine all ingredients.
2. Blend until all ingredients are thoroughly liquefied and combined, 30–60 seconds.
3. Consume immediately, or store with an airtight lid in the refrigerator for no more than 3–4 hours.

PER SERVING

CALORIES: 76	FAT: 1 G	PROTEIN: 3 G
SODIUM: 120 MG	FIBER: 5 G	
CARBOHYDRATES: 17 G		SUGAR: 8 G

Broccoli for Green Protein

With the addition of broccoli, you can improve the nutrition of any super smoothie. Packing protein, vitamin C, vitamin K, folate, and fiber, this cruciferous veggie cleanses the colon of debris, supports bone and muscle health, and helps keep you feeling full and focused for hours.

PROTEIN-PACKED PERFECTION

sweet

Along with the brain-boosting B vitamins that also improve energy levels, this fiber-filled super smoothie contains chia seeds and aloe vera juice. The result is long-lasting sustainable energy that makes this recipe the perfect protein-packed pick for a productive day.

18 OUNCES

½ banana, peeled and frozen
1 Bartlett pear, cored
1 tablespoon chia seeds
½ cup nonfat Greek yogurt
2 tablespoons aloe vera juice

1. In the 18-ounce NutriBullet cup, combine all ingredients.
2. Blend until all ingredients are thoroughly liquefied and combined, 30–60 seconds.
3. Consume immediately, or store with an airtight lid in the refrigerator for no more than 3–4 hours.

PER SERVING

CALORIES: 249	FAT: 5 G	PROTEIN: 7 G
SODIUM: 69 MG	FIBER: 8 G	
CARBOHYDRATES: 50 G		SUGAR: 32 G

SWEET SPLENDID GREENS

vegan, green, sweet

With all-natural sweetness, this super smoothie combines greens and fruits for a nutrient-dense cup that helps you maximize your energy levels and maintain those levels for hours. Complex carbohydrates, protein, and fiber provide your brain and body with the precise nutrition you need for a splendid day.

18 OUNCES

½ cup spinach
1 kale leaf
1 small Fuji apple, cored
½ banana, peeled and frozen
1 cup organic apple juice (see Introduction)

1. In the 18-ounce NutriBullet cup, combine all ingredients.
2. Blend until all ingredients are thoroughly liquefied and combined, 30–60 seconds.
3. Consume immediately, or store with an airtight lid in the refrigerator for no more than 3–4 hours.

PER SERVING

CALORIES: 233	FAT: 1 G	PROTEIN: 2 G
SODIUM: 22 MG	FIBER: 4 G	
CARBOHYDRATES: 59 G		SUGAR: 44 G

RAPID RASPBERRY REV-UP

vegan, sweet

Optimizing the rich antioxidants of raspberries, the naturally occurring oils and enzymes help to improve the body's metabolism, cleanse the body of toxins, and maximize energy levels. With a wide variety of vitamins, minerals, and phytochemicals that combine to create a super smoothie of maximum nutrition, you can rev up your day.

18 OUNCES

1 cup raspberries
¼" piece ginger, peeled
1 tablespoon aloe vera juice
1 tablespoon coconut oil
1 cup green tea, cooled

1. In the 18-ounce NutriBullet cup, combine all ingredients.
2. Blend until all ingredients are thoroughly liquefied and combined, 30–60 seconds.
3. Consume immediately, or store with an airtight lid in the refrigerator for no more than 3–4 hours.

PER SERVING

CALORIES: 184	FAT: 14 G	PROTEIN: 1 G
SODIUM: 1 MG	FIBER: 8 G	
CARBOHYDRATES: 15 G		SUGAR: 5 G

OMEGAS UNLEASHED

sweet

With powerful vitamins A, C, and E, plus iron, magnesium, and calcium, plus potent phytochemicals, carbohydrates, protein, and fat, this omega-rich super smoothie provides your body and mind with supportive nutrition that works synergistically for improved functioning, increased energy, and optimal health.

18 OUNCES

1 cup cherries

1 ounce walnuts

1 tablespoon ground flax seed

1 cup nonfat Greek yogurt

¼ cup red raspberry tea, cooled

1. In the 18-ounce NutriBullet cup, combine all ingredients.
2. Blend until all ingredients are thoroughly liquefied and combined, 30–60 seconds.
3. Consume immediately, or store with an airtight lid in the refrigerator for no more than 3–4 hours.

PER SERVING

CALORIES: 280	FAT: 19 G	PROTEIN: 6 G
SODIUM: 1 MG	FIBER: 5 G	
CARBOHYDRATES: 28 G		SUGAR: 20 G

BANANAS FOR BANANAS!

vegan, sweet, paleo

Potassium-rich bananas combine with protein-packed cashews, the omegas of flax seed, and antioxidants of two potent spices for a good-tasting treat that boosts brain functioning and increases energy levels and endurance.

18 OUNCES

2 bananas, peeled and frozen

1 ounce cashews

1 ounce ground flax seed

½ teaspoon ground cloves

½ teaspoon ground organic cinnamon

1 cup vanilla almond milk

1. In the 18-ounce NutriBullet cup, combine all ingredients.
2. Blend until all ingredients are thoroughly liquefied and combined, 30–60 seconds.
3. Consume immediately, or store with an airtight lid in the refrigerator for no more than 3–4 hours.

PER SERVING

CALORIES: 600	FAT: 26 G	PROTEIN: 20 G
SODIUM: 103 MG	FIBER: 17 G	
CARBOHYDRATES: 83 G		SUGAR: 38 G

Bananas Add Delicious Support for Heart Health

Bananas add more than creamy deliciousness to super smoothies—as a rich source of potassium, they support heart health. As one of the naturally sweetest fruits, this superfood packs tons of health-boosting nutrition and taste to any super smoothie. With B_6, manganese, calcium, potassium, boron, biotin, and copper working synergistically to maximize health benefits to all of the body's cells, systems, and functions, this superfruit is a nutritious and delicious way to achieve better health naturally.

SWEET POTATO PROTEIN PERFECTION

sweet

By combining the complex carbohydrates of sweet potatoes with the protein of walnuts and flax seed, and the healthy fat of yogurt, you can deliver all of the essential macronutrients to your brain and body. With the added support of brain-boosting omegas and antioxidants, this is one super smoothie that tastes great and makes you feel even greater.

18 OUNCES

½ sweet potato, cleaned thoroughly and skin intact

1 ounce walnuts

1 tablespoon ground flax seed

1 teaspoon ground organic cinnamon

½ cup low-fat Greek yogurt

½ cup vanilla almond milk

1. In the 18-ounce NutriBullet cup, combine all ingredients.

2. Blend until all ingredients are thoroughly liquefied and combined, 30–60 seconds.

3. Consume immediately, or store with an airtight lid in the refrigerator for no more than 3–4 hours.

PER SERVING

CALORIES: 335	FAT: 23 G	PROTEIN: 10 G
SODIUM: 92 MG	FIBER: 8 G	
CARBOHYDRATES: 27 G		SUGAR: 8 G

CACAO CURE FOR CHOCO CRAVINGS

sweet, paleo

When the craving for chocolate strikes, forgo the sugar-laden unhealthy processed options and opt for this smoothie instead. With rich flavors that mimic chocolate milk's depth, but pack quality nutrition that provides the body with brain-boosting benefits, this smoothie gives you sustainable energy and calms your chocolate cravings.

18 OUNCES

½ cup dates, pitted
1 banana, peeled and frozen
1 tablespoon raw cacao
2 teaspoons organic honey
1 cup vanilla almond milk

1. In the 18-ounce NutriBullet cup, combine all ingredients.
2. Blend until all ingredients are thoroughly liquefied and combined, 30–60 seconds.
3. Consume immediately, or store with an airtight lid in the refrigerator for no more than 3–4 hours.

PER SERVING

CALORIES: 498	FAT: 4 G	PROTEIN: 10 G
SODIUM: 98 MG	FIBER: 11 G	
CARBOHYDRATES: 115 G		SUGAR: 89 G

ENERGIZING ELIXIR

vegan, sweet

Antioxidants abound in every single ingredient in this smoothie. With sweet citrus, tart cherries, hydrating aloe, and light-tasting green tea, the flavors of this blend are only surpassed by the maximum nutritional benefits that result from every ingredient's vitamins, minerals, and phytochemicals.

18 OUNCES

½ red grapefruit, sectioned
1 tangerine, peeled
½ cup cherries, pitted
1 tablespoon aloe vera juice
1 cup green tea, cooled

1. In the 18-ounce NutriBullet cup, combine all ingredients.
2. Blend until all ingredients are thoroughly liquefied and combined, 30–60 seconds.
3. Consume immediately, or store with an airtight lid in the refrigerator for no more than 3–4 hours.

PER SERVING

CALORIES: 147	FAT: 1 G	PROTEIN: 3 G
SODIUM: 2 MG	FIBER: 5 G	
CARBOHYDRATES: 37 G		SUGAR: 30 G

PREPARE WITH PEARS!

sweet

When the body is provided with a combination of energy-improving carbohydrates, reparative protein, and healthy fats that assist in metabolism, energy levels rise naturally and are sustained for greater periods of time. Add plentiful vitamins, minerals, and phytochemicals, and this super smoothie is a potent blend of delicious nutrition.

18 OUNCES

2 Bartlett pears, cored

¼" piece ginger, peeled

½ cup nonfat Greek yogurt

¼ cup organic apple juice (see Introduction)

1. In the 18-ounce NutriBullet cup, combine all ingredients.
2. Blend until all ingredients are thoroughly liquefied and combined, 30–60 seconds.
3. Consume immediately, or store with an airtight lid in the refrigerator for no more than 3–4 hours.

PER SERVING

CALORIES: 227	FAT: 1 G	PROTEIN: 9 G
SODIUM: 14 MG	FIBER: 10 G	
CARBOHYDRATES: 58 G		SUGAR: 40 G

MAXIMUM RESULTS

vegan, green, sweet

Deep-green veggies get sweetened up with fiber-filled fruits in this energizing super smoothie. Helping to provide the brain and body with essential macro- and micronutrients, this blend of powerful nutrients improves brain functioning, supports physical endurance, and protects the cells throughout the brain and body for an optimal level of health.

18 OUNCES

¼ cup spinach
¼ cup pineapple
½ Fuji apple, cored
½ banana, peeled and frozen
1 tablespoon chia seeds
¾ cup green tea, cooled

1. In the 18-ounce NutriBullet cup, combine all ingredients.
2. Blend until all ingredients are thoroughly liquefied and combined, 30–60 seconds.
3. Consume immediately, or store with an airtight lid in the refrigerator for no more than 3–4 hours.

PER SERVING

CALORIES: 126	FAT: 5 G	PROTEIN: 3 G
SODIUM: 8 MG	FIBER: 3 G	
CARBOHYDRATES: 21 G		SUGAR: 11 G

WALNUT WONDER

vegan, sweet

This super smoothie has it all! Every ingredient ensures that your body's bones, muscles, nerves, and blood have the vitamins, minerals, omegas, antioxidants, and phytochemicals for optimal health, maximum performance, and better benefits.

18 OUNCES

1 banana, peeled and frozen
¼ cup raw rolled oats
1 tablespoon ground flax seed
1 tablespoon walnuts
1 tablespoon almonds
1 cup unsweetened vanilla almond milk

1. In the 18-ounce NutriBullet cup, combine all ingredients.
2. Blend until all ingredients are thoroughly liquefied and combined, 30–60 seconds.
3. Consume immediately, or store with an airtight lid in the refrigerator for no more than 3–4 hours.

PER SERVING

CALORIES: 492	FAT: 22 G	PROTEIN: 18 G
SODIUM: 97 MG	FIBER: 15 G	
CARBOHYDRATES: 62 G		SUGAR: 22 G

MUSCLE MOTIVATOR

vegan, green, sweet, paleo

These ingredients provide the brain and body with stimulation, energy, and sustainability, making this smoothie the perfect option for a pre-workout snack. Full of natural fiber-rich sweetness, this blend ensures that blood sugar levels remain stable so you stay motivated and energized for hours.

18 OUNCES

¼ cup spinach

1 kiwi

½ cup grapes

1 small Fuji apple, cored

1 cup organic apple juice (see Introduction)

1. In the 18-ounce NutriBullet cup, combine all ingredients.
2. Blend until all ingredients are thoroughly liquefied and combined, 30–60 seconds.
3. Consume immediately, or store with an airtight lid in the refrigerator for no more than 3–4 hours.

PER SERVING

CALORIES: 277	FAT: 1 G	PROTEIN: 2 G
SODIUM: 21 MG	FIBER: 4 G	
CARBOHYDRATES: 53 G		SUGAR: 36 G

CHAPTER 12

13 SMOOTHIES FOR PRE- AND POST-WORKOUT

With the right nutrition, you can maximize your workouts for better benefits to your entire body. Helping to improve muscle strength, support bone health, maximize metabolic functioning, and regulate hormone levels, quality nutrition can help you use workouts for optimal health. By adding the smoothies listed in this chapter to your daily diet, you can boost your energy levels, sustain that energy for longer periods of time, and help your body recover from workouts in ways that benefit every cell and system.

These smoothies contain complex carbohydrates, protein, and healthy fats in combination with essential vitamins, minerals, and phytochemicals from nutrient-dense superfoods. Supporting the entire body's intricate systems and parts, these delicious recipes revitalize, rejuvenate, and protect with quality nutrition that will help you transform your health and your life.

YUMMY YAZZBERRY YOGURT

sweet

Beautiful berries combine with kefir and almond milk for a sweet treat that provides complex carbohydrates, protein, and healthy fats. These macronutrients plus the plentiful vitamins, minerals, and antioxidants in every ingredient supply the body with the nutrition it needs for sustained energy, strength, and repair.

18 OUNCES

½ cup strawberries
½ cup blueberries
½ cup raspberries
½ cup low-fat vanilla kefir
½ cup vanilla almond milk

1. In the 18-ounce NutriBullet cup, combine all ingredients.
2. Blend until all ingredients are thoroughly liquefied and combined, 30–60 seconds.
3. Consume immediately, or store with an airtight lid in the refrigerator for no more than 3–4 hours.

PER SERVING

CALORIES: 153	FAT: 3 G	PROTEIN: 5 G
SODIUM: 50 MG	FIBER: 8 G	
CARBOHYDRATES: 30 G		SUGAR: 18 G

Spices for Maximized Metabolism

When you add spiciness to your smoothies, snacks, and meals, the benefits don't stop at intense taste sensations. Within those spicy foods such as ginger and hot peppers, and warm spices such as turmeric and cayenne, natural phytochemicals not only heat up your taste buds but also rev up your metabolism. With what's called a thermogenic effect, these additions actually heat up your body, burning fat and calories, while requiring your body to burn even more calories to return your body's temperature to normal.

BLASTING BERRIES

vegan, sweet

Violet blackberries provide a hydrating hit of valuable nutrition in this smoothie that packs protective antioxidants in every sip. With vitamins, minerals, and phytochemicals that deliver essential nutrition to the entire body, this delicious blend of slightly sweet and refreshing flavors comes with a blast of benefits.

18 OUNCES

½ cup blackberries
½ cup watermelon
½ small cucumber
1 tablespoon aloe vera juice
½ cup green tea, cooled

1. In the 18-ounce NutriBullet cup, combine all ingredients.
2. Blend until all ingredients are thoroughly liquefied and combined, 30–60 seconds.
3. Consume immediately, or store with an airtight lid in the refrigerator for no more than 3–4 hours.

PER SERVING

CALORIES: 76	FAT: 1 G	PROTEIN: 1 G
SODIUM: 5 MG	FIBER: 5 G	
CARBOHYDRATES: 18 G		SUGAR: 11 G

AMAZING AMINOS

sweet

Amino acids are essential when it comes to preparing for or recovering from an intense workout. Helping to deliver a powerhouse performance to the cells, this smoothie is a great combination of macro- and micronutrients that support the body's synthesis and metabolism of protein for revved-up energy, rapid recovery, and optimized results.

18 OUNCES

1 banana, peeled and frozen
½ cup blueberries
¼ cup pineapple
1 cup nonfat Greek yogurt
2 tablespoons aloe vera juice

1. In the 18-ounce NutriBullet cup, combine all ingredients.
2. Blend until all ingredients are thoroughly liquefied and combined, 30–60 seconds.
3. Consume immediately, or store with an airtight lid in the refrigerator for no more than 3–4 hours.

PER SERVING

CALORIES: 179	FAT: 1 G	PROTEIN: 9 G
SODIUM: 18 MG	FIBER: 5 G	
CARBOHYDRATES: 43 G		SUGAR: 26 G

PERFECT PEACHY PROTEIN

vegan, sweet, paleo

Creamy, delicious, and nutritious, this smoothie combines the sweet flavors of beta-carotene-rich peaches and potassium-packed bananas with protein-fueled cashews and almond milk. The result supports the bones, muscles, blood, and brain for increased energy, sustained strength, and maximum results.

18 OUNCES

2 peaches, pitted
½ banana, peeled and frozen
1 ounce raw cashews
1 cup almond milk

1. In the 18-ounce NutriBullet cup, combine all ingredients.
2. Blend until all ingredients are thoroughly liquefied and combined, 30–60 seconds.
3. Consume immediately, or store with an airtight lid in the refrigerator for no more than 3–4 hours.

PER SERVING

CALORIES: 453	FAT: 17 G	PROTEIN: 16 G
SODIUM: 127 MG	FIBER: 8 G	
CARBOHYDRATES: 65 G		SUGAR: 43 G

ENERGETIC GREENS

vegan, green, sweet

Fueling your workouts with fiber has never been sweeter. This simple smoothie combines delicious green veggies with apple, hydrating cucumber, and antioxidant-rich green tea for a natural energy-boosting pre-workout snack or meal that supports and protects the cells of the body.

18 OUNCES

½ cup spinach
1 kale leaf
1 Granny Smith apple, cored
1 small cucumber
½ cup green tea, cooled

1. In the 18-ounce NutriBullet cup, combine all ingredients.
2. Blend until all ingredients are thoroughly liquefied and combined, 30–60 seconds.
3. Consume immediately, or store with an airtight lid in the refrigerator for no more than 3–4 hours.

PER SERVING

CALORIES: 139	FAT: 1 G	PROTEIN: 4 G
SODIUM: 30 MG	FIBER: 4 G	
CARBOHYDRATES: 35 G		SUGAR: 21 G

RASPBERRIES FOR RECOVERY

sweet

Sweet and slightly tart, this smoothie packs vitamins, minerals, and antioxidants along with omegas, protein, carbohydrates, and healthy fats into every sip for intense nutrition that yields rapid results. Providing your muscles and bones with the support they need after a workout, this delicious blend of nutrient-dense fruits and additions makes for a speedy recovery with rapid results.

18 OUNCES

1½ cups raspberries
1 tablespoon lemon juice
1 cup nonfat Greek yogurt
1 tablespoon ground flax seed
1 teaspoon organic honey

1. In the 18-ounce NutriBullet cup, combine all ingredients.
2. Blend until all ingredients are thoroughly liquefied and combined, 30–60 seconds.
3. Consume immediately, or store with an airtight lid in the refrigerator for no more than 3–4 hours.

PER SERVING

CALORIES: 167	FAT: 4 G	PROTEIN: 9 G
SODIUM: 5 MG	FIBER: 12 G	
CARBOHYDRATES: 29 G		SUGAR: 14 G

BERRY BLASTS FOR MUSCLE MASS

sweet

Using the fiber and rich nutrition of berries plus protein-packed flax seed and yogurt, this beautiful and tasty smoothie delivers lactic acid–relieving nutrition to the muscles that helps them repair and rebuild, stronger and healthier than before!

18 OUNCES

½ cup blueberries

½ cup blackberries

1 tablespoon ground flax seed

½ cup nonfat Greek yogurt

½ cup red raspberry tea, cooled

1. In the 18-ounce NutriBullet cup, combine all ingredients.
2. Blend until all ingredients are thoroughly liquefied and combined, 30–60 seconds.
3. Consume immediately, or store with an airtight lid in the refrigerator for no more than 3–4 hours.

PER SERVING

CALORIES: 113	FAT: 3 G	PROTEIN: 13 G
SODIUM: 10 MG	FIBER: 8 G	
CARBOHYDRATES: 21 G		SUGAR: 12 G

CULINARY CREATIONS FOR "CUTS"

vegan, sweet

Those defining lines of muscle striations that every avid exerciser seeks can be achieved through hard work and a clean diet. This smoothie supports your diet by providing energizing nutrition that improves metabolism, burns fat deposits, and hydrates and rejuvenates muscle cells. Astoundingly nutritious, this cool fat-burning combination can help you see definition.

18 OUNCES

1 cup watermelon
½ cup cubed cantaloupe
1 small tangerine, peeled
2 tablespoons aloe vera juice
½ cup green tea, cooled

1. In the 18-ounce NutriBullet cup, combine all ingredients.
2. Blend until all ingredients are thoroughly liquefied and combined, 30–60 seconds.
3. Consume immediately, or store with an airtight lid in the refrigerator for no more than 3–4 hours.

PER SERVING

CALORIES: 112	FAT: 1 G	PROTEIN: 2 G
SODIUM: 16 MG	FIBER: 3 G	
CARBOHYDRATES: 28 G		SUGAR: 24 G

GREAT GRAPE RECOVERY

vegan, sweet, paleo

The healthy hydration of grapes and pears combines with the benefits of their natural polyphenols for drastic improvement throughout the body. Protecting every cell in the body from toxic oxidative stress, this super smoothie not only provides fiber for increased sustained energy for improved workouts but also supports the rejuvenation and repair of cells for youthfulness on the inside and out.

18 OUNCES

1 cup grapes, frozen

1 Bartlett pear, cored

1 cup organic apple juice (see Introduction)

1 tablespoon aloe vera juice

1. In the 18-ounce NutriBullet cup, combine all ingredients.
2. Blend until all ingredients are thoroughly liquefied and combined, 30–60 seconds.
3. Consume immediately, or store with an airtight lid in the refrigerator for no more than 3–4 hours.

PER SERVING

CALORIES: 315	FAT: 1 G	PROTEIN: 2 G
SODIUM: 15 MG	FIBER: 7 G	
CARBOHYDRATES: 81 G		SUGAR: 64 G

TROPICAL YUMMY YOGURT

sweet

A sweet treat that boosts workout benefits is every clean eater's dream come true. With nutrient-dense fruits that pack a punch of flavor while providing energizing B vitamins, protective vitamin C and antioxidants, and reparative protein, this tropical treat encourages the optimal functioning of all of the body's systems so you can stay fast, fit, and focused.

18 OUNCES

½ cup pineapple

1 banana, peeled and frozen

1 kiwi

1 tangerine, peeled

1 cup nonfat Greek yogurt

1. In the 18-ounce NutriBullet cup, combine all ingredients.
2. Blend until all ingredients are thoroughly liquefied and combined, 30–60 seconds.
3. Consume immediately, or store with an airtight lid in the refrigerator for no more than 3–4 hours.

PER SERVING

CALORIES: 262	FAT: 1 G	PROTEIN: 8 G
SODIUM: 8 MG	FIBER: 8 G	
CARBOHYDRATES: 64 G		SUGAR: 34 G

NUTS ABOUT PROTEIN

vegan, sweet, paleo

Clean protein from natural sources such as nuts helps to fuel the body's muscles. Add brain-boosting potassium to that protein, and you've got a prescription for quality nutrition that sharpens focus, improves energy and endurance, and helps to speed recovery and maximize results. All of these benefits from a sweet and simple super smoothie? What could be better?

18 OUNCES

2 bananas, peeled and frozen

1 ounce walnuts

1 ounce cashews

1 tablespoon ground flax seed

½ cup vanilla almond milk

1. In the 18-ounce NutriBullet cup, combine all ingredients.
2. Blend until all ingredients are thoroughly liquefied and combined, 30–60 seconds.
3. Consume immediately, or store with an airtight lid in the refrigerator for no more than 3–4 hours.

PER SERVING

CALORIES: 632	FAT: 36 G	PROTEIN: 17 G
SODIUM: 54 MG	FIBER: 12 G	
CARBOHYDRATES: 74 G		SUGAR: 35 G

BROCCOLI BLEND

vegan, savory

Fueling workouts, maximizing metabolism, and increasing satisfaction with a feeling of fullness that lasts, the fiber in this super smoothie helps you to achieve physical greatness with every savory sip.

18 OUNCES

1 cup broccoli florets

1 tomato

1 garlic clove

1 tablespoon chopped red onion

1 cup green tea, cooled

1. In the 18-ounce NutriBullet cup, combine all ingredients.
2. Blend until all ingredients are thoroughly liquefied and combined, 30–60 seconds.
3. Consume immediately, or store with an airtight lid in the refrigerator for no more than 3–4 hours.

PER SERVING

CALORIES: 261	FAT: 1 G	PROTEIN: 4 G
SODIUM: 37 MG	FIBER: 4 G	
CARBOHYDRATES: 13 G		SUGAR: 5 G

CREAMY, DREAMY SWEETNESS

sweet

This smoothie combines the perfect blend of superfoods and spices for maximum benefits to the brain and body. With complex carbohydrates, protein, and healthy fats, this naturally sweet treat provides it all—helping the body to metabolize nutrients efficiently, maximizing and supporting the health of the blood, brain, bones, and muscles.

18 OUNCES

2 bananas

1 teaspoon ground organic cinnamon

½ teaspoon ground cloves

2 tablespoons aloe vera juice

1 cup nonfat Greek yogurt

1. In the 18-ounce NutriBullet cup, combine all ingredients.
2. Blend until all ingredients are thoroughly liquefied and combined, 30–60 seconds.
3. Consume immediately, or store with an airtight lid in the refrigerator for no more than 3–4 hours.

PER SERVING

CALORIES: 231	FAT: 1 G	PROTEIN: 9 G
SODIUM: 5 MG	FIBER: 8 G	
CARBOHYDRATES: 56 G		SUGAR: 29 G

CHAPTER 13

14 SMOOTHIES FOR BETTER BRAIN FUNCTION

Imagine waking up feeling refreshed and with full energy, moving through your day feeling focused and alert, finding yourself with improved memory and attention, less mental fog, and fewer "lulls." In short, imagine that your brain functions better throughout the entire day. With the right nutrition, this can be your reality. That nutrition includes vitamins such as Bs, C, and E; minerals such as iron, magnesium, potassium, manganese, zinc, and calcium; and of course protective and preventative nutrients like omegas, antioxidants, anti-inflammatories, proteins, fats, and carbohydrates. They're all included in this chapter's smoothie recipes!

BLUEBERRIES FOR BRAIN HEALTH

sweet

Antioxidants of blueberries are a special protective kind that helps to prevent oxidative stress and damage to brain cells. These natural polyphenols called anthocyanins help support brain health and improve nerve functioning for long-lasting brain benefits. This smoothie combines these brain-boosting berries with nutritious and delicious additions for a potent blend of perfection you can sip any time.

18 OUNCES

1 cup blueberries
½ cup nonfat Greek yogurt
3 tablespoons aloe vera juice
¼" piece ginger, peeled

1. In the 18-ounce NutriBullet cup, combine all ingredients.
2. Blend until all ingredients are thoroughly liquefied and combined, 30–60 seconds.
3. Consume immediately, or store with an airtight lid in the refrigerator for no more than 3–4 hours.

PER SERVING

CALORIES: 90	FAT: 0 G	PROTEIN: 8 G
SODIUM: 10 MG	FIBER: 4 G	
CARBOHYDRATES: 21 G		SUGAR: 15 G

A Word about Antioxidants

From blueberries to flax seeds, tomatoes to eggplant, and ginger to cinnamon, the foods you love can provide your body and mind with powerful antioxidant protection against cell degradation, cancerous changes within cells and organs, and even improved immunity against bacterial, viral, and microbial infections.

FATS FOR FIT BRAINS

sweet

With "fit" or healthy fats that help the conduction of nerve cells' messages, the brain and body can experience synergistic benefits that boost the functioning of every organ system and process. This smoothie's ingredients combine naturally fit-fat-packed nuts with sweet bananas and creamy yogurt for a brain-healthy treat you can sip as a snack or a meal.

18 OUNCES

1 banana, peeled and frozen
1 ounce walnuts
1 ounce cashews
½ cup full-fat vanilla yogurt
1 tablespoon ground flax seed
2 tablespoons aloe vera juice

1. In the 18-ounce NutriBullet cup, combine all ingredients.
2. Blend until all ingredients are thoroughly liquefied and combined, 30–60 seconds.
3. Consume immediately, or store with an airtight lid in the refrigerator for no more than 3–4 hours.

PER SERVING

CALORIES: 581	FAT: 35 G	PROTEIN: 18 G
SODIUM: 85 MG	FIBER: 8 G	
CARBOHYDRATES: 58 G		SUGAR: 34 G

FIT FATS FOR NERVE FUNCTIONING

sweet

The fit fats of natural sources such as mangoes, avocados, and yogurt help support the nerves in a number of ways. Protecting and improving these systemic essentials is a priority. This smoothie's fit fats, rich antioxidants, and wide array of vitamins and minerals combine to provide perfect protection against illness and disease that can wreak havoc on the nerves, brain, and body.

18 OUNCES

½ banana, peeled and frozen

½ mango

1 kiwi

1 small avocado, pitted and with skin removed

½ cup full-fat vanilla Greek yogurt

1 tablespoon ground flax seed

3 tablespoons aloe vera juice

1. In the 18-ounce NutriBullet cup, combine all ingredients.
2. Blend until all ingredients are thoroughly liquefied and combined, 30–60 seconds.
3. Consume immediately, or store with an airtight lid in the refrigerator for no more than 3–4 hours.

PER SERVING

CALORIES: 562	FAT: 34 G	PROTEIN: 10 G
SODIUM: 76 MG	FIBER: 19 G	
CARBOHYDRATES: 65 G		SUGAR: 29 G

Brain-Boosting Nutrients

Much like the muscles' demand for protein and the skin's requirement for hydrating nutrients, the brain needs particular nutrients to thrive. Vitamins and minerals including calcium, potassium, zinc, magnesium, B vitamins, vitamin C, vitamin A, and vitamin K as well as protective antioxidants all help the brain to function, rejuvenate, repair, and remain protected.

HONEYDEW FOR HAPPY THOUGHTS

vegan, sweet, paleo

These fiber-filled melons and antioxidant-packed fruits combine with oil- and enzyme-rich ginger to help regulate blood sugar and hormone production. This in turn aids in improving mood and reducing fluctuations in emotion. With tasty flavors, this hydrating super smoothie is a mood mender that you can enjoy anytime to make a happier experience out of your day.

18 OUNCES

1 cup cubed honeydew, room temperature
1 tablespoon coconut oil
1 kiwi
¼" piece ginger, peeled
½ cup green tea, cooled

1. In the 18-ounce NutriBullet cup, combine all ingredients.
2. Blend until all ingredients are thoroughly liquefied and combined, 30–60 seconds.
3. Consume immediately, or store with an airtight lid in the refrigerator for no more than 3–4 hours.

PER SERVING

CALORIES: 227	FAT: 14 G	PROTEIN: 2 G
SODIUM: 34 MG	FIBER: 4 G	
CARBOHYDRATES: 27 G		SUGAR: 14 G

SPARKLING STRAWBERRY

vegan, sweet

Spiced perfectly, this blend of beautiful berries, stimulating cloves, invigorating ginger, and naturally caffeinated antioxidant-rich green tea makes for an energizing elixir that not only tastes great but improves mood. Through stimulation of the senses, this smoothie's scrumptious ingredients not only make for a visual, tasty, and aromatic treat that helps energize your brain, but the smoothie's variety of vitamins and minerals also enhance energy and increase focus and clarity.

18 OUNCES

1 cup strawberries, frozen
¼ teaspoon ground cloves
¼" piece ginger, peeled
2 tablespoons aloe vera juice
1 cup green tea, cooled

1. In the 18-ounce NutriBullet cup, combine all ingredients.
2. Blend until all ingredients are thoroughly liquefied and combined, 30–60 seconds.
3. Consume immediately, or store with an airtight lid in the refrigerator for no more than 3–4 hours.

PER SERVING

CALORIES: 48	FAT: 1 G	PROTEIN: 1 G
SODIUM: 3 MG	FIBER: 3 G	
CARBOHYDRATES: 11 G		SUGAR: 7 G

MANGOES FOR MOODINESS

sweet

Beta-carotene-rich mango combines with tasty vitamin C–concentrated tangerine and protein-packed yogurt for a fiber-filled super smoothie that stimulates the senses, calms cravings, and satisfies nutritional needs. All of this comes in a sweet blend of delicious nutrition that you can enjoy as a guilt-free snack or meal any time you need a quick pick-me-up.

18 OUNCES

1 cup mango

1 tangerine, peeled

½ cup nonfat Greek yogurt

¼ cup organic apple juice (see Introduction)

1 tablespoon aloe vera juice

1. In the 18-ounce NutriBullet cup, combine all ingredients.
2. Blend until all ingredients are thoroughly liquefied and combined, 30–60 seconds.
3. Consume immediately, or store with an airtight lid in the refrigerator for no more than 3–4 hours.

PER SERVING

CALORIES: 200	FAT: 1 G	PROTEIN: 9 G
SODIUM: 16 MG	FIBER: 5 G	
CARBOHYDRATES: 50 G		SUGAR: 42 G

CS FOR COGNITION

vegan, sweet

Improving focus while optimizing health sounds like a big job, but combining energizing citrus fruits in antioxidant-rich green tea with enzyme-packed aloe vera gets that job done. Light and refreshing but packed with flavor, this super smoothie supports brain functioning while protecting brain cells against degradation and disease.

18 OUNCES

1 cup strawberries
1 tangerine, peeled
1 kiwi
½ cup pineapple
½ cup green tea, cooled
1 tablespoon aloe vera juice

1. In the 18-ounce NutriBullet cup, combine all ingredients.
2. Blend until all ingredients are thoroughly liquefied and combined, 30–60 seconds.
3. Consume immediately, or store with an airtight lid in the refrigerator for no more than 3–4 hours.

PER SERVING

CALORIES: 191	FAT: 1 G	PROTEIN: 3 G
SODIUM: 8 MG	FIBER: 9 G	
CARBOHYDRATES: 48 G		SUGAR: 27 G

GREENS FOR GREATER THINKING

vegan, green, sweet

With vitamin C, vitamin K, iron, potassium, antioxidants, and anti-inflammatory compounds, this sweet green treat is a good way to support every aspect of the nervous system. It gives you quality nutrition that helps improve nerve health, support cardiovascular functioning, maintain brain tissue health, and encourage speedy communication between nerve cells throughout the body.

18 OUNCES

½ cup spinach
1 kale leaf
1 banana, peeled and frozen
1 kiwi
1 cup green tea, cooled

1. In the 18-ounce NutriBullet cup, combine all ingredients.
2. Blend until all ingredients are thoroughly liquefied and combined, 30–60 seconds.
3. Consume immediately, or store with an airtight lid in the refrigerator for no more than 3–4 hours.

PER SERVING

CALORIES: 155	FAT: 1 G	PROTEIN: 2 G
SODIUM: 17 MG	FIBER: 6 G	
CARBOHYDRATES: 39 G		SUGAR: 14 G

FRUITS AND FLAX SEED

sweet

Fiber-filled fruits combine with omega-rich flax seed and protein-packed yogurt for a nutrient-dense super smoothie that benefits the brain and body. Supporting the cells, organs, and systems of the body, these delicious and nutritious ingredients improve functioning, boost immunity, and promote overall health in every last sip.

18 OUNCES

1 banana, peeled and frozen
1 Fuji apple, cored
1 tablespoon ground flax seed
½ cup nonfat Greek yogurt
2 tablespoons aloe vera juice

1. In the 18-ounce NutriBullet cup, combine all ingredients.
2. Blend until all ingredients are thoroughly liquefied and combined, 30–60 seconds.
3. Consume immediately, or store with an airtight lid in the refrigerator for no more than 3–4 hours.

PER SERVING

CALORIES: 223	FAT: 3 G	PROTEIN: 9 G
SODIUM: 9 MG	FIBER: 7 G	
CARBOHYDRATES: 51 G		SUGAR: 32 G

OMEGAS FOR OPTIMAL BRAIN FUNCTIONING

sweet

Packed with antioxidants, this super smoothie provides for and protects a brain that functions at its best. This blend of ingredients provides the brain with protective phytochemicals that safeguard the nervous system from illness and disease, all while supplying the entire body with essential nutrients that further support the brain's and body's overall health.

18 OUNCES

1 banana, peeled and frozen
1 tangerine, peeled
1 ounce walnuts
1 tablespoon ground flax seed
½ cup nonfat Greek yogurt
3 tablespoons aloe vera juice

1. In the 18-ounce NutriBullet cup, combine all ingredients.
2. Blend until all ingredients are thoroughly liquefied and combined, 30–60 seconds.
3. Consume immediately, or store with an airtight lid in the refrigerator for no more than 3–4 hours.

PER SERVING

CALORIES: 386	FAT: 22 G	PROTEIN: 9 G
SODIUM: 12 MG	FIBER: 9 G	
CARBOHYDRATES: 49 G		SUGAR: 28 G

PEACHY PROTECTION

sweet

Vibrant beta-carotene-rich peaches combine with potassium-packed bananas and protein-rich yogurt in this brain-healthy super smoothie. With the added benefits of omegas, antioxidants, and anti-inflammatory compounds, this sweet treat becomes a powerful potion of protection to keep the brain healthy and happy.

18 OUNCES

1 banana, peeled and frozen
1 peach, pitted
1 tablespoon ground flax seed
2 tablespoons aloe vera juice
½ cup nonfat Greek yogurt

1. In the 18-ounce NutriBullet cup, combine all ingredients.
2. Blend until all ingredients are thoroughly liquefied and combined, 30–60 seconds.
3. Consume immediately, or store with an airtight lid in the refrigerator for no more than 3–4 hours.

PER SERVING

CALORIES: 202	FAT: 3 G	PROTEIN: 12 G
SODIUM: 9 MG	FIBER: 8 G	
CARBOHYDRATES: 44 G		SUGAR: 27 G

PURPLE PEACHES FOR PREVENTION

vegan, sweet

The bright colors of this super smoothie's ingredients signify their intense nutrition and immense benefits. With anthocyanins, beta-carotene, oils, enzymes, and antioxidants, these sweet and spicy ingredients unite to provide the brain with a sweet treat of protective nutrition that also energizes and optimizes functioning.

18 OUNCES

1 peach, pitted

1 cup Concord grapes

¼" piece ginger, peeled

½ cup green tea, cooled

1. In the 18-ounce NutriBullet cup, combine all ingredients.
2. Blend until all ingredients are thoroughly liquefied and combined, 30–60 seconds.
3. Consume immediately, or store with an airtight lid in the refrigerator for no more than 3–4 hours.

PER SERVING

CALORIES: 185	FAT: 1 G	PROTEIN: 3 G
SODIUM: 5 MG	FIBER: 4 G	
CARBOHYDRATES: 46 G		SUGAR: 35 G

THE PERFECT PROTEIN PRESCRIPTION

sweet

Ingredients for this smoothie contain natural complex carbohydrates that provide the cells with fuel, protein sources that support the cells' functioning and repair, and antioxidants that protect those cells from damage and disease. They all combine to provide the brain and body with everything it needs to remain fit and focused for hours, and healthy for years to come.

18 OUNCES

1 banana, peeled and frozen
1 tablespoon raw rolled oats
1 tablespoon ground flax seed
1 ounce walnuts
½ cup low-fat Greek yogurt
¼ cup vanilla almond milk

1. In the 18-ounce NutriBullet cup, combine all ingredients.
2. Blend until all ingredients are thoroughly liquefied and combined, 30–60 seconds.
3. Consume immediately, or store with an airtight lid in the refrigerator for no more than 3–4 hours.

PER SERVING

CALORIES: 440	FAT: 26 G	PROTEIN: 14 G
SODIUM: 80 MG	FIBER: 8 G	
CARBOHYDRATES: 45 G		SUGAR: 23 G

KIWIS FOR CREATIVITY

vegan, sweet

The vitamin C content of this smoothie is through the roof! With vibrant citrus fruits and sweet strawberries, this colorful combination of vitamin C–packed produce makes for a super smoothie that enhances energy, stimulates the senses, improves immunity, and safeguards the brain's and body's overall health.

18 OUNCES

½ cup strawberries
½ cup pineapple
2 kiwis
1 cup orange sections

1. In the 18-ounce NutriBullet cup, combine all ingredients.
2. Blend until all ingredients are thoroughly liquefied and combined, 30–60 seconds.
3. Consume immediately, or store with an airtight lid in the refrigerator for no more than 3–4 hours.

PER SERVING

CALORIES: 242	FAT: 1 G	PROTEIN: 4 G
SODIUM: 9 MG	FIBER: 12 G	
CARBOHYDRATES: 60 G		SUGAR: 28 G

CHAPTER 14

14 SMOOTHIES FOR TOTAL HEALTH

Using nutrient-dense superfoods in your NutriBullet's super smoothies, you can improve your body's overall health. The antioxidant-rich fruits, vegetables, and additions combine to provide your body with protection against illness and disease, while improving the health and optimizing the functioning of the body's parts and systems. Supported with an abundance of quality nutrients including protein, complex carbohydrates, and healthy fats, as well as vitamins, minerals, and unique phytochemicals, these delicious super smoothies help you achieve total health.

Because busy schedules and costly ingredients sometimes derail the best intentions to get healthy, we designed these super smoothies to use the best ingredients in a combination that requires little time, effort, and cost. Anyone, regardless of lifestyle, can enjoy the benefits of better health. The ingredients in these recipes can be found at any grocery store or local market.

CANCER COMBATANT

sweet

Delicious citrus fruits combine with kefir and hydrating aloe vera in this smoothie for a cup full of protective vitamin C and antioxidants, anti-inflammatory agents, valuable vitamins and minerals, and potent phytochemicals. All of these provide protection against free radical damage.

18 OUNCES

2 kiwis
½ cup pineapple
1 cup low-fat kefir
2 tablespoons aloe vera juice

1. In the 18-ounce NutriBullet cup, combine all ingredients.
2. Blend until all ingredients are thoroughly liquefied and combined, 30–60 seconds.
3. Consume immediately, or store with an airtight lid in the refrigerator for no more than 3–4 hours.

PER SERVING

CALORIES: 268	FAT: 8 G	PROTEIN: 7 G
SODIUM: 8 MG	FIBER: 6 G	
CARBOHYDRATES: 33 G		SUGAR: 8 G

Chronic Conditions Cure

With chronic disease able to wreak havoc on cells, tissues, organs, and systems, it is absolutely imperative to provide your body with the nutrients and phytochemicals it needs to prevent, treat, and reverse oxidative damage that can lead to those debilitating changes. Drinking super smoothies containing plenty of antioxidants, anti-inflammatory agents, and unique enzymes and oils can help you safeguard your system and cells from chronic conditions effectively and naturally.

ANTIOXIDANT ALLEVIATOR

vegan, sweet

Every single food in this super smoothie delivers powerful antioxidant protection to keep your immune system running at its best and your cells protected from harm. Sweet and simple, this berry citrus blend is great as a light snack or a meal.

18 OUNCES

½ cup blueberries
½ cup raspberries
¼ cup pineapple
1 cup green tea, cooled

1. In the 18-ounce NutriBullet cup, combine all ingredients.
2. Blend until all ingredients are thoroughly liquefied and combined, 30–60 seconds.
3. Consume immediately, or store with an airtight lid in the refrigerator for no more than 3–4 hours.

PER SERVING

CALORIES: 95	FAT: 1 G	PROTEIN: 2 G
SODIUM: 2 MG	FIBER: 6 G	
CARBOHYDRATES: 23 G		SUGAR: 14 G

RESPIRATORY RELIEF

vegan, sweet

Potent polyphenols such as anthocyanins not only give these berries their brilliant colors but also help to relieve respiratory distress by opening airways, combating toxins, and protecting all of the body's cells against damage. Improving health while protecting the lungs and all of the respiratory system's fragile components, this super smoothie will help you breathe easy.

18 OUNCES

½ cup blueberries
½ cup blackberries
¼" piece ginger, peeled
1 cup green tea, cooled
2 tablespoons aloe vera juice

1. In the 18-ounce NutriBullet cup, combine all ingredients.
2. Blend until all ingredients are thoroughly liquefied and combined, 30–60 seconds.
3. Consume immediately, or store with an airtight lid in the refrigerator for no more than 3–4 hours.

PER SERVING

CALORIES: 73	FAT: 1 G	PROTEIN: 2 G
SODIUM: 1 MG	FIBER: 6 G	
CARBOHYDRATES: 18 G		SUGAR: 11 G

COOL COLON CLEANSER

sweet

A cleansed colon remains free of toxic debris. It also can house beneficial bacteria that fight off infections within the gut and improve overall immune system function. With fiber-rich fruits and beneficial additions such as kefir and flax seed, this super smoothie is one that will keep you happy and healthy.

18 OUNCES

1 banana, peeled and frozen
½ cup pineapple
½ cup strawberries
½ cup low-fat vanilla kefir
1 tablespoon ground flax seed

1. In the 18-ounce NutriBullet cup, combine all ingredients.
2. Blend until all ingredients are thoroughly liquefied and combined, 30–60 seconds.
3. Consume immediately, or store with an airtight lid in the refrigerator for no more than 3–4 hours.

PER SERVING

CALORIES: 210	FAT: 3 G	PROTEIN: 4 G
SODIUM: 4 MG	FIBER: 8 G	
CARBOHYDRATES: 46 G		SUGAR: 26 G

ALL-HEALING ALOE

vegan, green, sweet, paleo

The foods in this smoothie possess some of the most nutrient-dense quality nutrition available. Combining vitamin C–rich kiwis with protein-plentiful spirulina and antioxidant- and anti-inflammatory-packed aloe and green tea, this super smoothie is a simple way to gain greater health with less illness, better system functioning, and protected cell health.

18 OUNCES

2 kiwis

1 teaspoon spirulina

¼ cup aloe vera juice

¾ cup green tea, cooled

1. In the 18-ounce NutriBullet cup, combine all ingredients.
2. Blend until all ingredients are thoroughly liquefied and combined, 30–60 seconds.
3. Consume immediately, or store with an airtight lid in the refrigerator for no more than 3–4 hours.

PER SERVING

CALORIES: 93	FAT: 1 G	PROTEIN: 2 G
SODIUM: 8 MG	FIBER: 5 G	
CARBOHYDRATES: 23 G		SUGAR: 0 G

Diabetes Diets

Diabetes is a dangerous disease that can seriously impact all aspects of life. It requires an especially clean diet of natural foods that don't trigger blood sugar spikes and dips, and are able to help a diabetic person maintain stable blood sugar levels and proper hormone balance. With the addition of spices and extracts such as ginger and aloe vera, you can naturally improve the diabetic condition while increasing the deliciousness of natural snacks and meals.

EDEN ELIXIR

vegan, sweet

This elixir is a simple and easy way to get quality nutrition that not only tastes sensational but provides every cell with rich antioxidants that serve and protect. Supply your body with enzymes that help produce and utilize macronutrients, store and spread micronutrients, and maximize the benefits of protective phytochemicals.

18 OUNCES

1 Fuji apple, cored
1 cup blueberries
2 tablespoons aloe vera juice
1 cup green tea, cooled

1. In the 18-ounce NutriBullet cup, combine all ingredients.
2. Blend until all ingredients are thoroughly liquefied and combined, 30–60 seconds.
3. Consume immediately, or store with an airtight lid in the refrigerator for no more than 3–4 hours.

PER SERVING

CALORIES: 161	FAT: 1 G	PROTEIN: 2 G
SODIUM: 1 MG	FIBER: 6 G	
CARBOHYDRATES: 42 G		SUGAR: 31 G

POWERHOUSE-A-PLENTY

sweet

Vitamin C, B vitamins, iron, magnesium, potassium, antioxidants, anti-inflammatory agents, probiotics, and unique enzymes combine in this smoothie for the perfect protective powerhouse combo of nutrients delivered in a sweet and creamy snack or meal that you're sure to love.

18 OUNCES

1 peach, pitted

½ banana, peeled and frozen

½ cup strawberries

½ cup low-fat vanilla kefir

2 tablespoons aloe vera juice

1 teaspoon ground organic cinnamon

1. In the 18-ounce NutriBullet cup, combine all ingredients.
2. Blend until all ingredients are thoroughly liquefied and combined, 30–60 seconds.
3. Consume immediately, or store with an airtight lid in the refrigerator for no more than 3–4 hours.

PER SERVING

CALORIES: 144	FAT: 2 G	PROTEIN: 3 G
SODIUM: 2 MG	FIBER: 6 G	
CARBOHYDRATES: 35 G		SUGAR: 23 G

TROPICAL TOP-NOTCH TWIST

vegan, sweet, paleo

The taste of the tropics has never been more delicious . . . or more beneficial! With pineapple and kiwi, natural coconut, hydrating aloe, and coconut oil rich in medium-chain fatty acids, this coconut-milk-based super smoothie is a simple way to better your body and your mind.

18 OUNCES

½ cup pineapple
½ cup raw coconut meat
1 kiwi
2 tablespoons aloe vera juice
1 tablespoon coconut oil
½ cup nonfat coconut milk

1. In the 18-ounce NutriBullet cup, combine all ingredients.
2. Blend until all ingredients are thoroughly liquefied and combined, 30–60 seconds.
3. Consume immediately, or store with an airtight lid in the refrigerator for no more than 3–4 hours.

PER SERVING

CALORIES: 571	FAT: 51 G	PROTEIN: 5 G
SODIUM: 27 MG	FIBER: 7 G	
CARBOHYDRATES: 31 G		SUGAR: 11 G

SWEET CELERY CELEBRATION

vegan, sweet

A sweet spin on a savory favorite, this smoothie blends fruits with hydrating celery and cucumber in antioxidant-rich green tea. You get a splendid taste sensation that provides protective phytochemicals and essential vitamins and minerals in every vibrant drop.

18 OUNCES

1 celery stalk
½ cucumber
1 kiwi
½ Bartlett pear, cored
1 cup green tea, cooled

1. In the 18-ounce NutriBullet cup, combine all ingredients.
2. Blend until all ingredients are thoroughly liquefied and combined, 30–60 seconds.
3. Consume immediately, or store with an airtight lid in the refrigerator for no more than 3–4 hours.

PER SERVING

CALORIES: 123	FAT: 1 G	PROTEIN: 2 G
SODIUM: 40 MG	FIBER: 7 G	
CARBOHYDRATES: 31 G		SUGAR: 11 G

GRAPES FOR GREAT HEALTH

vegan, sweet

The deep hue of this smoothie signifies the rich nutrition that includes plenty of vitamins, minerals, and phytochemicals. With anthocyanidins, anthocyanins, bromelain, gingerol, and unique enzymes and oils, this delicious treat is one of the most antioxidant-rich super smoothies. It not only protects brain and body health, but it's also delicious beyond belief.

18 OUNCES

1 cup Concord grapes, frozen
½ cup pineapple
¼" piece ginger, peeled
2 tablespoons aloe vera juice
1 cup green tea, cooled

1. In the 18-ounce NutriBullet cup, combine all ingredients.
2. Blend until all ingredients are thoroughly liquefied and combined, 30–60 seconds.
3. Consume immediately, or store with an airtight lid in the refrigerator for no more than 3–4 hours.

PER SERVING

CALORIES: 145	FAT: 0 G	PROTEIN: 2 G
SODIUM: 4 MG	FIBER: 3 G	
CARBOHYDRATES: 38 G		SUGAR: 32 G

HYDRATING HONEYDEW

vegan, sweet

The hydrating ingredients included in this simple smoothie penetrate the body's cells with nutrition that you can see as well as feel. Helping to nourish the skin, cells, organs, and systems, this combination of delicious foods packs vitamins, minerals, and antioxidants into every sip for a supercharged smoothie of health-transforming protection and support.

18 OUNCES

1 cup cubed honeydew
½ cucumber
½ kiwi
½ cup green tea, cooled

1. In the 18-ounce NutriBullet cup, combine all ingredients.
2. Blend until all ingredients are thoroughly liquefied and combined, 30–60 seconds.
3. Consume immediately, or store with an airtight lid in the refrigerator for no more than 3–4 hours.

PER SERVING

CALORIES: 106	FAT: 1 G	PROTEIN: 1 G
SODIUM: 35 MG	FIBER: 3 G	
CARBOHYDRATES: 27 G		SUGAR: 16 G

VERY CHERRY YOGURT PARFAIT

sweet

The perfect parfait of a smoothie is this combination of phytochemical-rich cherries, anti-inflammatory aloe vera, and omega-packed flax seed, blended with the healthy carbohydrates of oats and essential servings of calcium and protein from yogurt. This smoothie supports the body's and mind's overall health while supplying long-lasting energy.

18 OUNCES

1 cup cherries, pitted
2 tablespoons aloe vera juice
1 tablespoon ground flax seed
¼ cup raw rolled oats
¾ cup nonfat Greek yogurt

1. In the 18-ounce NutriBullet cup, combine all ingredients.
2. Blend until all ingredients are thoroughly liquefied and combined, 30–60 seconds.
3. Consume immediately, or store with an airtight lid in the refrigerator for no more than 3–4 hours.

PER SERVING

CALORIES: 280	FAT: 5 G	PROTEIN: 13 G
SODIUM: 100 MG	FIBER: 7 G	
CARBOHYDRATES: 53 G		SUGAR: 32 G

SIMPLE SAVORY SMOOTHIE

vegan, savory

Sometimes you need a little spice in your life, and it's those times that call for this savory super smoothie. Fiber-rich veggies that provide vitamins, minerals, and protective antioxidants combine in this surprisingly light blend of superfoods that improve overall health and maximize wellness with every savory sip.

18 OUNCES

1 medium tomato

1 tablespoon chopped red onion

1 celery stalk

1 garlic clove

1 cup green tea, cooled

1. In the 18-ounce NutriBullet cup, combine all ingredients.
2. Blend until all ingredients are thoroughly liquefied and combined, 30–60 seconds.
3. Consume immediately, or store with an airtight lid in the refrigerator for no more than 3–4 hours.

PER SERVING

CALORIES: 37	FAT: 0 G	PROTEIN: 2 G
SODIUM: 39 MG	FIBER: 2 G	
CARBOHYDRATES: 8 G		SUGAR: 4 G

ORANGE PROTECTION AND PREVENTION

sweet

With beta-carotene, antioxidants, anti-inflammatory agents, carbohydrates, protein, and fat, along with an array of vitamins and minerals, this sweet treat is a relaxing way to enjoy the nutrition that gives your body the support it needs while protecting against illness and disease.

18 OUNCES

1 medium sweet potato, cleaned thoroughly and skin intact

2 tablespoons raw rolled oats

1 teaspoon ground organic cinnamon

½ teaspoon ground cardamom

½ teaspoon ground cloves

3 tablespoons aloe vera juice

½ cup nonfat Greek yogurt

1. In the 18-ounce NutriBullet cup, combine all ingredients.
2. Blend until all ingredients are thoroughly liquefied and combined, 30–60 seconds.
3. Consume immediately, or store with an airtight lid in the refrigerator for no more than 3–4 hours.

PER SERVING

CALORIES: 210	FAT: 4 G	PROTEIN: 8 G
SODIUM: 141 MG	FIBER: 7 G	
CARBOHYDRATES: 44 G		SUGAR: 14 G

CHAPTER 15

14 SMOOTHIES FOR WOMEN'S HEALTH

There's nothing better than sweet treats that also help the brain and body become healthier. This chapter's smoothies are dedicated to maximizing the health benefits to the female body through nutrient-dense superfoods that taste great and provide your body with everything it wants and needs. Every recipe is both nutritious and good-tasting to the last drop! Now you can indulge in delicious treats without guilt because you're providing your body with the cleanest, most potent nutrition available.

The female body requires different nutrients at different times for various functions; these super smoothies are designed to deliver the perfect blends of superfoods tailored to a woman's needs. Whether you're looking for the perfect recipe for fitness, fertility, pregnancy, PMS or menopause relief, energy, sleep, or overall health and wellness, you'll find a smoothie that works for you.

Optimizing Nutrition Benefits with Ginger

By using the naturally occurring phytochemicals of ginger, you can unharness immense nutritional benefits to your entire body from foods you already include in your daily diet. With the simple addition of ginger, your smoothies and other snacks and meals become supercharged with oils, enzymes, and phytonutrients that help your body to process and utilize the nutrients of the other ingredients you choose.

YUMMY MENOPAUSE MIXER

vegan, sweet

Given the fluctuations that come with menopause, the smartest priority is to base your nutrition on satisfying the needs of the systems and organs associated with hormones. With antioxidants, medium-chain fatty acids, soothing polyphenols, and active enzymes that all work synergistically to regulate hormones, improve cognitive functioning, maintain stable moods, and improve sleep quality, every ingredient in this delicious super smoothie helps to support the body's intricate systems for a better menopause experience.

18 OUNCES

1 cup raspberries

1 cup cubed honeydew

¼" piece ginger, peeled

2 tablespoons aloe vera juice

½–¾ cup red raspberry tea, cooled

1. In the 18-ounce NutriBullet cup, combine all ingredients.
2. Blend until all ingredients are thoroughly liquefied and combined, 30–60 seconds.
3. Consume immediately, or store with an airtight lid in the refrigerator for no more than 3–4 hours.

PER SERVING

CALORIES: 125	FAT: 1 G	PROTEIN: 2 G
SODIUM: 32 MG	FIBER: 9 G	
CARBOHYDRATES: 30 G		SUGAR: 19 G

BERRY BLEND FOR BONE HEALTH

sweet

This blend of berries and rich yogurt is a strong supporter of women's health against osteoporosis, packing bone-building nutrition into every last drop! Providing essential nutrients like B vitamins, A, C, and E, as well as essential calcium and magnesium, this delicious and nutritious blend of superfoods creates a spectacular super smoothie that promotes overall health and protects against the degradation of bone mass.

18 OUNCES

½ cup raspberries
½ cup blueberries
½ cup pineapple
1 cup nonfat Greek yogurt

1. In the 18-ounce NutriBullet cup, combine all ingredients.
2. Blend until all ingredients are thoroughly liquefied and combined, 30–60 seconds.
3. Consume immediately, or store with an airtight lid in the refrigerator for no more than 3–4 hours.

PER SERVING

CALORIES: 211	FAT: 1 G	PROTEIN: 10 G
SODIUM: 134 MG	FIBER: 7 G	
CARBOHYDRATES: 134 G		SUGAR: 35 G

PREGNANCY PERFECTION

sweet

The perfect pregnancy potion packs vital vitamins and minerals, fiber, folate, protein, and complex carbohydrates that help to support the growth of both mom and baby. Sip yourself to better health while providing your body and your baby with all they need to be strong and healthy.

18 OUNCES

½ cup blueberries

½ cup strawberries

½ banana, peeled and frozen

½ cup nonfat Greek yogurt

¼ cup red raspberry tea, cooled

1. In the 18-ounce NutriBullet cup, combine all ingredients.
2. Blend until all ingredients are thoroughly liquefied and combined, 30–60 seconds.
3. Consume immediately, or store with an airtight lid in the refrigerator for no more than 3–4 hours.

PER SERVING

CALORIES: 165	FAT: 1 G	PROTEIN: 6 G
SODIUM: 68 MG	FIBER: 5 G	
CARBOHYDRATES: 38 G		SUGAR: 27 G

MORNING SICKNESS MENDER

vegan, sweet

This mix of simple ingredients not only provides the perfect potion for relieving morning sickness symptoms, but also packs tons of vital nutrition into one simple snack or meal. You can restore and rejuvenate the organs, systems, and cells that may have been deprived of valuable nutrients when your troubled tummy was turned off by foods. Helping to calm the nerves, regulate hormone fluctuations, and improve digestion, this blend of superfoods helps ease tummy troubles naturally.

18 OUNCES

1½ cups strawberries

¼" piece ginger, peeled

1 teaspoon honey

½ teaspoon ground organic cinnamon

1 cup red raspberry tea, cooled

1. In the 18-ounce NutriBullet cup, combine all ingredients.
2. Blend until all ingredients are thoroughly liquefied and combined, 30–60 seconds.
3. Consume immediately, or store with an airtight lid in the refrigerator for no more than 3–4 hours.

PER SERVING

CALORIES: 135	FAT: 1 G	PROTEIN: 2 G
SODIUM: 3 MG	FIBER: 5 G	
CARBOHYDRATES: 23 G		SUGAR: 16 G

SWEET PMS SAVIOR

sweet

Helping to relieve the physical and mental symptoms of the dreaded premenstrual syndrome, this sweet treat provides vitamin C, potassium, calcium, antioxidants, anti-inflammatory agents, healthy fats, and protein, for a super smoothie that combats bloating, water retention, fatigue, and moodiness.

18 OUNCES

1 cup strawberries
1 banana, peeled and frozen
½ cup pineapple
½ cup nonfat Greek yogurt
2 tablespoons aloe vera juice

1. In the 18-ounce NutriBullet cup, combine all ingredients.
2. Blend until all ingredients are thoroughly liquefied and combined, 30–60 seconds.
3. Consume immediately, or store with an airtight lid in the refrigerator for no more than 3–4 hours.

PER SERVING

CALORIES: 198	FAT: 1 G	PROTEIN: 10 G
SODIUM: 3 MG	FIBER: 7 G	
CARBOHYDRATES: 49 G		SUGAR: 30 G

BERRY-BANANA BLOAT-BUSTER

vegan, sweet

Bloating can be frustrating and uncomfortable, but you can easily relieve it by using hydrating nutrients that help restore health to the body's systems. With vitamins, minerals, and antioxidants, this delicious blend of superfoods helps rehydrate and rejuvenate the cells while restoring balance to the bloodstream and helping normalize the hormonal fluctuations that contributed to bloating.

18 OUNCES

½ cup raspberries

½ banana, peeled and frozen

½ cup pineapple

1 cup red raspberry tea, cooled

1. In the 18-ounce NutriBullet cup, combine all ingredients.
2. Blend until all ingredients are thoroughly liquefied and combined, 30–60 seconds.
3. Consume immediately, or store with an airtight lid in the refrigerator for no more than 3–4 hours.

PER SERVING

CALORIES: 126	FAT: 1 G	PROTEIN: 2 G
SODIUM: 2 MG	FIBER: 7 G	
CARBOHYDRATES: 32 G		SUGAR: 18 G

FATIGUE FIGHTER

sweet

An assortment of fruits combine with calcium- and protein-packed yogurt in this smoothie for a supportive blend of superfoods that supplies the body and mind with essential nutrients that fight fatigue, ignite energy, and sustain that newfound power for hours.

18 OUNCES

1 clementine, peeled
½ cup pineapple
½ banana, peeled and frozen
1 kiwi
½ cup nonfat Greek yogurt

1. In the 18-ounce NutriBullet cup, combine all ingredients.
2. Blend until all ingredients are thoroughly liquefied and combined, 30–60 seconds.
3. Consume immediately, or store with an airtight lid in the refrigerator for no more than 3–4 hours.

PER SERVING

CALORIES: 203	FAT: 1 G	PROTEIN: 11 G
SODIUM: 16 MG	FIBER: 7 G	
CARBOHYDRATES: 51 G		SUGAR: 28 G

BETTER BREAST HEALTH

vegan, green, sweet

With calcium, iron, vitamin K, vitamin E, vitamin C, and powerful phytochemicals, this blend helps protect breast health with valuable nutrients proven to keep cancer and disease at bay. Helping to fight inflammation and protect against oxidative stress and damage, this delicious super smoothie is a beautiful blend of breast health protection.

18 OUNCES

½ cup spinach
1 kiwi
½ cup raspberries
½ cup pineapple
1 teaspoon honey
1 cup green tea, cooled

1. In the 18-ounce NutriBullet cup, combine all ingredients.
2. Blend until all ingredients are thoroughly liquefied and combined, 30–60 seconds.
3. Consume immediately, or store with an airtight lid in the refrigerator for no more than 3–4 hours.

PER SERVING

CALORIES: 145	FAT: 1 G	PROTEIN: 2 G
SODIUM: 17 MG	FIBER: 8 G	
CARBOHYDRATES: 36 G		SUGAR: 16 G

MUSCLE-MAINTAINING NUT-MILK

vegan, sweet, paleo

Muscles and bones help to support the framework of the entire body. They are an essential element of our physical system. In this smoothie the NutriBullet unharnesses protein, omegas, vitamins, and minerals to promote muscle and bone health.

18 OUNCES

1 cup dates, pitted

1 ounce cashews

1 tablespoon ground flax seed

1 cup unsweetened vanilla almond milk

1. In the 18-ounce NutriBullet cup, combine all ingredients.
2. Blend until all ingredients are thoroughly liquefied and combined, 30–60 seconds.
3. Consume immediately, or store with an airtight lid in the refrigerator for no more than 3–4 hours.

PER SERVING

CALORIES: 791	FAT: 19 G	PROTEIN: 17 G
SODIUM: 102 MG	FIBER: 18 G	
CARBOHYDRATES: 154 G		SUGAR: 121 G

OH, MAMA! OMEGAS!

vegan, sweet, paleo

The brain and body both benefit from the immense nutrition unleashed from every food in this super smoothie! With omega-rich flax seed and walnuts, antioxidant- and fiber-filled dates, clean carbohydrates from oats, and protein-packed flax milk, this delightful blend of superb nutrition helps a woman of any age enjoy better health.

18 OUNCES

1 banana, peeled and frozen
½ cup dates, pitted
1 ounce walnuts
1 tablespoon raw rolled oats
1 tablespoon ground flax seed
1 cup flax milk

1. In the 18-ounce NutriBullet cup, combine all ingredients.
2. Blend until all ingredients are thoroughly liquefied and combined, 30–60 seconds.
3. Consume immediately, or store with an airtight lid in the refrigerator for no more than 3–4 hours.

PER SERVING

CALORIES: 724	FAT: 26 G	PROTEIN: 18 G
SODIUM: 127 MG	FIBER: 16 G	
CARBOHYDRATES: 118 G		SUGAR: 81 G

KIWI CLARITY

vegan, green, sweet

This super smoothie combines vitamin C–rich kiwi, vitamin K- and iron-packed spinach, potassium-heavy bananas, and enzyme-loaded aloe with the plentiful antioxidants of green tea for a light and refreshing fibrous blend of fruits and veggies that keep a woman's brain running like a clean machine.

18 OUNCES

1 kiwi

½ cup spinach

½ banana, peeled and frozen

2 tablespoons aloe vera juice

1 cup green tea, cooled

1. In the 18-ounce NutriBullet cup, combine all ingredients.
2. Blend until all ingredients are thoroughly liquefied and combined, 30–60 seconds.
3. Consume immediately, or store with an airtight lid in the refrigerator for no more than 3–4 hours.

PER SERVING

CALORIES: 102	FAT: 1 G	PROTEIN: 2 G
SODIUM: 16 MG	FIBER: 4 G	
CARBOHYDRATES: 25 G		SUGAR: 7 G

SWEET DREAMS

vegan, sweet

Insomnia is a frustrating condition that can quickly wreak havoc on a woman's body and mind. With this super smoothie's combination of soothing fiber-filled fruits that add slight sweetness to calming chamomile and relaxing aloe vera, you can drift off into slumber sweetly.

18 OUNCES

1 banana, peeled and frozen
½ Fuji apple, cored
1 cup chamomile tea, cooled
2 tablespoons aloe vera juice
½ teaspoon ground organic cinnamon

1. In the 18-ounce NutriBullet cup, combine all ingredients.
2. Blend until all ingredients are thoroughly liquefied and combined, 30–60 seconds.
3. Consume immediately, or store with an airtight lid in the refrigerator for no more than 3–4 hours.

PER SERVING

CALORIES: 146	FAT: 1 G	PROTEIN: 2 G
SODIUM: 1 MG	FIBER: 5 G	
CARBOHYDRATES: 38 G		SUGAR: 23 G

VEGGIES FOR VISION

vegan, green, sweet

Illness and disease don't stand a chance against this onslaught of B vitamins, vitamins A, C, E, and K, iron, magnesium, calcium, and potent antioxidants. Combining this blend of superfoods into a super smoothie makes it easy to sip quality nutrition that protects the brain, body, and especially your eyes against degradation and damage.

18 OUNCES

½ cup spinach

2 carrots, greens removed, chopped

½ sweet potato, cleaned thoroughly and skin intact

1 cup green tea, cooled

½ teaspoon ground cloves

1. In the 18-ounce NutriBullet cup, combine all ingredients.
2. Blend until all ingredients are thoroughly liquefied and combined, 30–60 seconds.
3. Consume immediately, or store with an airtight lid in the refrigerator for no more than 3–4 hours.

PER SERVING

CALORIES: 122	FAT: 1 G	PROTEIN: 3 G
SODIUM: 150 MG	FIBER: 7 G	
CARBOHYDRATES: 28 G		SUGAR: 10 G

ANTIOXIDANTS GALORE!

vegan, sweet, paleo

Natural cacao is one of the most antioxidant-rich foods in the world. Combine it with potassium-packed bananas, omega-rich walnuts and flax seed, and fiber-filled dates in almond milk and you've got a potent smoothie that you can enjoy to the last drop.

18 OUNCES

1 banana, peeled and frozen

1 ounce walnuts

1 tablespoon ground flax seed

1 teaspoon ground organic cacao

½ cup dates

1 cup vanilla almond milk

1. In the 18-ounce NutriBullet cup, combine all ingredients.
2. Blend until all ingredients are thoroughly liquefied and combined, 30–60 seconds.
3. Consume immediately, or store with an airtight lid in the refrigerator for no more than 3–4 hours.

PER SERVING

CALORIES: 834	FAT: 38 G	PROTEIN: 21 G
SODIUM: 99 MG	FIBER: 19 G	
CARBOHYDRATES: 115 G		SUGAR: 79 G

CHAPTER 16

14 SMOOTHIES FOR MEN'S HEALTH

In order to keep the male body looking good, feeling great, and healthy for years to come, the focus on a clean diet should be top priority. Supporting the brain, bones, muscles, blood, and entire body with high-quality, clean, nutrient-dense foods is the most effective way to optimize system functioning, improve immunity, and maintain overall health. With valuable nutrients such as vitamins, minerals, and phytochemicals added to the essential proteins, complex carbohydrates, and healthy fats the body needs to survive, any man can improve his strength, energy levels, stamina, mental clarity, and immunity, and start living a new, healthier lifestyle of looking good, feeling great, and loving life.

With simple and easy super smoothies made using the ultra-efficient NutriBullet, these delicious and nutritious recipes can be made as a meal or a snack that you can even drink on the go! Packing in essential nutrients from delicious superfoods, these smoothies will keep you coming back for more. Start living a life of health that you want and deserve.

POMEGRANATE FOR PROSTATE

sweet

With unique phytochemicals that have been shown to slow the growth of cancerous cells in the prostate, pomegranate jewels are the perfect addition to any smoothie intended to support men's health. Combine them with probiotic-rich kefir for improved immunity, and you've got a sweet treat of superfoods that make every sip beneficial.

18 OUNCES

1 cup pomegranate jewels
1 cup low-fat kefir
1 teaspoon honey
2 tablespoons aloe vera juice

1. In the 18-ounce NutriBullet cup, combine all ingredients.
2. Blend until all ingredients are thoroughly liquefied and combined, 30–60 seconds.
3. Consume immediately, or store with an airtight lid in the refrigerator for no more than 3–4 hours.

PER SERVING

CALORIES: 300	FAT: 7 G	PROTEIN: 7 G
SODIUM: 7 MG	FIBER: 7 G	
CARBOHYDRATES: 40 G		SUGAR: 31 G

Popping Out Pomegranate Jewels Like a Pro

Cut a pomegranate in half and hold the halved fruit with the jewels facing down over a large bowl. Take a wooden spoon in the opposite hand and slap the fruit, unhinging the jewels from the fruit's flesh. In less than a minute, you can rotate the fruits, pop out the jewels, and do the same to the remaining half.

FATIGUE ZAPPER

vegan, sweet

Fighting fatigue with naturally energizing ingredients, this super smoothie combines sweet cherries, spicy ginger, naturally caffeinated green tea, and the natural enzymes and nutrients of aloe vera for a fatigue-fighting combination that will rejuvenate your body and mind.

18 OUNCES

1½ cups cherries, pitted

1 cup green tea, cooled

¼" piece ginger, peeled

2 tablespoons aloe vera juice

1. In the 18-ounce NutriBullet cup, combine all ingredients.
2. Blend until all ingredients are thoroughly liquefied and combined, 30–60 seconds.
3. Consume immediately, or store with an airtight lid in the refrigerator for no more than 3–4 hours.

PER SERVING

CALORIES: 146	FAT: 0 G	PROTEIN: 2 G
SODIUM: 0 MG	FIBER: 5 G	
CARBOHYDRATES: 37 G		SUGAR: 30 G

MOOD MAXIMIZER

sweet

All-natural ingredients combine in this B-vitamin-packed super smoothie for a delicious way to bring your mood back to normal. Improving energy, focus, mental functioning, and stamina, this nutrient-dense combination of carbohydrates, protein, vitamins, minerals, and phytochemicals helps support every cell, system, and function in the body so you can enjoy a healthier, happier existence.

18 OUNCES

2 small Fuji apples, cored

¼ cup raw rolled oats

½ cup low-fat honey kefir

1 teaspoon ground organic cinnamon

1 tablespoon coconut oil

½ cup organic apple juice (see Introduction)

1. In the 18-ounce NutriBullet cup, combine all ingredients.
2. Blend until all ingredients are thoroughly liquefied and combined, 30–60 seconds.
3. Consume immediately, or store with an airtight lid in the refrigerator for no more than 3–4 hours.

PER SERVING

CALORIES: 391	FAT: 15 G	PROTEIN: 10 G
SODIUM: 7 MG	FIBER: 7 G	
CARBOHYDRATES: 64 G		SUGAR: 40 G

BERRIES FULL OF BS

sweet

With beautiful berries that provide B vitamins, antioxidants, and fiber, this light and refreshing, satisfying smoothie combines foods that pack immense nutrition and flavor into every last sip. Energizing pineapple, banana, and kefir help berries deliver maximum nutrition for maximum benefits to the body and mind.

18 OUNCES

½ cup strawberries
½ cup blueberries
½ cup pineapple
½ banana, peeled and frozen
1 cup low-fat kefir

1. In the 18-ounce NutriBullet cup, combine all ingredients.
2. Blend until all ingredients are thoroughly liquefied and combined, 30–60 seconds.
3. Consume immediately, or store with an airtight lid in the refrigerator for no more than 3–4 hours.

PER SERVING

CALORIES: 291	FAT: 8 G	PROTEIN: 10 G
SODIUM: 5 MG	FIBER: 6 G	
CARBOHYDRATES: 43 G		SUGAR: 28 G

BRAIN-BOOSTING "CHOCOLATE" MILK FOR TWO!

vegan, sweet, paleo

It's not like any other chocolate milk you've ever had. This supercharged smoothie uses raw cacao powder to unharness one of the most antioxidant-rich superfoods on the planet. Full of natural brain-boosting benefits, it supports and protects brain health and functioning. I highly recommend that you share this smoothie or separate it into two servings to be consumed at different times.

18 OUNCES

1 cup dates, pitted
1 banana, peeled and frozen
¼ cup raw rolled oats
1 tablespoon ground flax seed
1 tablespoon raw cacao powder
1 cup almond milk

1. In the 18-ounce NutriBullet cup, combine all ingredients.
2. Blend until all ingredients are thoroughly liquefied and combined, 30–60 seconds.
3. Consume immediately, or store with an airtight lid in the refrigerator for no more than 3–4 hours.
4. If reserving half the smoothie to be consumed at a later time, the reserved portion can be frozen for 5–7 days.

PER SERVING

CALORIES: 718	FAT: 5 G	PROTEIN: 11 G
SODIUM: 6 MG	FIBER: 21 G	
CARBOHYDRATES: 177 G		SUGAR: 127 G

MUSCLE MAXIMIZER

sweet

Delivering complex carbohydrates, protein, vitamins, minerals, and phytochemicals directly into the bloodstream, every sip of this delicious smoothie unleashes the power of potent phytochemicals that support muscle health. You can enjoy sustained energy and rapid recovery for a strength you can see and feel like never before!

18 OUNCES

1 sweet potato, cleaned thoroughly, skin intact
¼ cup raw rolled oats
½ cup nonfat Greek yogurt
½ cup almond milk
2 tablespoons aloe vera juice
1 teaspoon ground organic cinnamon

1. In the 18-ounce NutriBullet cup, combine all ingredients.
2. Blend until all ingredients are thoroughly liquefied and combined, 30–60 seconds.
3. Consume immediately, or store with an airtight lid in the refrigerator for no more than 3–4 hours.

PER SERVING

CALORIES: 249	FAT: 1 G	PROTEIN: 9 G
SODIUM: 122 MG	FIBER: 7 G	
CARBOHYDRATES: 45 G		SUGAR: 8 G

FRUITY FOCUS FIXER

sweet

Fatigue can attack the body and mind. When your fatigued focus needs fixing, look no further than this taste sensation! This smoothie's antioxidant-rich blueberries, fiber-filled bananas, omega-packed flax seed, and clean protein-fueled yogurt deliver essential nutrition to the brain for optimized functioning and improved focus all day.

18 OUNCES

1 cup blueberries

½ banana, peeled and frozen

½ cup nonfat Greek yogurt

1 tablespoon ground flax seed

½ cup organic apple juice (see Introduction)

1. In the 18-ounce NutriBullet cup, combine all ingredients.
2. Blend until all ingredients are thoroughly liquefied and combined, 30–60 seconds.
3. Consume immediately, or store with an airtight lid in the refrigerator for no more than 3–4 hours.

PER SERVING

CALORIES: 234	FAT: 3 G	PROTEIN: 7 G
SODIUM: 15 MG	FIBER: 8 G	
CARBOHYDRATES: 52 G		SUGAR: 34 G

PRUNES FOR PREVENTION

vegan, green, sweet

With colon cancer and digestive issues topping the charts for health concerns among men, preventative colon care is an imperative. Combining fiber-rich ingredients such as prunes, apples, and spinach that cleanse the colon while contributing an array of vitamins, minerals, and antioxidants, this smoothie will keep your colon clean and protected against illness and disease.

18 OUNCES

1 cup prunes, pitted
½ Fuji apple, cored
½ cup spinach
1 teaspoon ground organic cinnamon
¼ teaspoon ground cloves
1 cup green tea, cooled

1. In the 18-ounce NutriBullet cup, combine all ingredients.
2. Blend until all ingredients are thoroughly liquefied and combined, 30–60 seconds.
3. Consume immediately, or store with an airtight lid in the refrigerator for no more than 3–4 hours.

PER SERVING

CALORIES: 457	FAT: 1 G	PROTEIN: 4 G
SODIUM: 17 MG	FIBER: 14 G	
CARBOHYDRATES: 121 G		SUGAR: 73 G

Prunes for Colon-Cleansing Immunity-Boosting Benefits

Since the majority of the immune system's support stems from the gut, it's no wonder that fiber-rich fruits such as prunes can help sweep clean the colon's tract and support the immune system's functioning. With the cleansing fibrous gel it produces, the prune's natural fibrous material scrapes toxins and debris from the intestinal tract while delivering powerful antioxidants.

MEN'S MENTAL MENDER

vegan, green, savory

Keeping you full and focused, this smoothie's B vitamins and vitamins A, C, E, and K, along with minerals including potassium, iron, and calcium, work synergistically to deliver essential nutrients to the brain and nerves while also helping to maintain stable blood sugar and hormone levels, all of which promote healthy brain functioning and fight mental fogginess.

18 OUNCES

½ teaspoon spirulina
¼ cup broccoli
½ tomato
1 celery stalk
½ cucumber
¼ cup spinach
1 garlic clove
1 cup green tea, cooled

1. In the 18-ounce NutriBullet cup, combine all ingredients.
2. Blend until all ingredients are thoroughly liquefied and combined, 30–60 seconds.
3. Consume immediately, or store with an airtight lid in the refrigerator for no more than 3–4 hours.

PER SERVING

CALORIES: 54	FAT: 0 G	PROTEIN: 3 G
SODIUM: 52 MG	FIBER: 3 G	
CARBOHYDRATES: 12 G		SUGAR: 5 G

Better Brain Functioning

The brain and nervous system rely heavily on the vitamins and minerals consumed in the diet, so it's easy to see how you can adapt your diet for better brain functioning. By focusing your snacks and meals on vibrant foods such as leafy greens, beautiful berries, creamy bananas, refreshing citrus, and omega-rich additions, you can deliver potent nutrition to the brain that help it stay functioning at its best.

STRAWBERRIES FOR STAMINA

sweet

The vitamin C of strawberries does double duty in this delicious smoothie by supporting the immune system and protecting against free radical damage. When it comes to stamina, this protection is vital, since the cardiovascular system and heart are the powerhouse players that contribute to sustained energy levels.

18 OUNCES

1 cup strawberries

¼" piece ginger, peeled

1 cup low-fat kefir

3 tablespoons aloe vera juice

1 teaspoon ground organic cinnamon

1 teaspoon ground cloves

1. In the 18-ounce NutriBullet cup, combine all ingredients.
2. Blend until all ingredients are thoroughly liquefied and combined, 30–60 seconds.
3. Consume immediately, or store with an airtight lid in the refrigerator for no more than 3–4 hours.

PER SERVING

CALORIES: 194	FAT: 8 G	PROTEIN: 8 G
SODIUM: 101 MG	FIBER: 5 G	
CARBOHYDRATES: 14 G		SUGAR: 14 G

Clean Diet Makes for Clean Bodies and Clear Minds

Processed foods that stay "fresh" for months or years in packages, cans, or boxes can cause blood sugar level fluctuations, hormonal imbalances, and brain chemical irregularities that all wreak havoc on your focus, mental clarity, and energy levels. On the other hand, a clean diet focused on natural foods provides your brain with essential nutrients and uplifting phytochemicals that can help your brain function at its best.

SWEET SEXUAL HEALTH

vegan, sweet, paleo

Blood flow, blood health, and cardiovascular functioning play major roles in sexual health. Each benefits immensely from this smoothie's combination of delicious superfoods. With protective antioxidants, cleansing enzymes, and essential vitamins and minerals that keep the heart strong, this is a delicious way to improve your sexual health.

18 OUNCES

1 sweet potato, cleaned thoroughly, skin intact
½ banana, peeled and frozen
1 ounce cashews
1 tablespoon ground flax seed
1 cup almond milk
1 teaspoon cardamom

1. In the 18-ounce NutriBullet cup, combine all ingredients.
2. Blend until all ingredients are thoroughly liquefied and combined, 30–60 seconds.
3. Consume immediately, or store with an airtight lid in the refrigerator for no more than 3–4 hours.

PER SERVING

CALORIES: 459	FAT: 19 G	PROTEIN: 15 G
SODIUM: 171 MG	FIBER: 10 G	
CARBOHYDRATES: 61 G		SUGAR: 21 G

Spice Up Your Sex Life

Naturally warm spices such as ginger, cinnamon, and cardamom can actually improve your sex life by stimulating your senses, raising your blood pressure, and triggering the release of brain chemicals in the same way as when you experience arousal. With the simple addition of spice, you can also improve blood flow throughout the body, improve stamina, and regulate hormones and blood pressure more efficiently for an improved performance in the bedroom.

HEART HEALTH HELPER

vegan, savory

Every savory sip of this smoothie provides protective nutrients and phytochemicals directly into the bloodstream and heart thanks to the extractor blades of the NutriBullet. Nutrients such as vitamins A, C, E, and K, iron, calcium, magnesium, and potassium (many of which double as powerful antioxidants) are found in these superfoods. They replenish, rejuvenate, and protect, improving the health and functioning of every intricate part of the most important network in your body.

18 OUNCES

½ cup spinach
1 kale leaf
½ small tomato
½ avocado, pitted and with skin removed
1 garlic clove
2 tablespoons aloe vera juice
1 cup purified water

1. In the 18-ounce NutriBullet cup, combine all ingredients.
2. Blend until all ingredients are thoroughly liquefied and combined, 30–60 seconds.
3. Consume immediately, or store with an airtight lid in the refrigerator for no more than 3–4 hours.

PER SERVING

CALORIES: 210	FAT: 15 G	PROTEIN: 5 G
SODIUM: 50 MG	FIBER: 9 G	
CARBOHYDRATES: 18 G		SUGAR: 2 G

SPICY SICKNESS SOOTHER

vegan, savory, paleo

When you're down with a slight or serious infection, it can be hard to consume the right nutrition for fighting off illness. With the vitamins, minerals, antioxidants, oils, and enzymes in this smoothie, your body will be equipped to fight bacteria, viruses, and microbes. At the same time, the smoothie delivers antiseptic, anti-inflammatory, and analgesic compounds throughout the body.

18 OUNCES

¼" piece ginger, peeled
1½ cups green tea, warm
1 tablespoon apple cider vinegar
½ tablespoon coconut oil
2 tablespoons aloe vera juice

1. In the 18-ounce NutriBullet cup, combine all ingredients.
2. Blend until all ingredients are thoroughly liquefied and combined, 30–60 seconds.
3. Consume immediately, or store with an airtight lid in the refrigerator for no more than 3–4 hours.

PER SERVING

CALORIES: 63	FAT: 7 G	PROTEIN: 0 G
SODIUM: 1 MG	FIBER: 0 G	
CARBOHYDRATES: 0 G		SUGAR: 0 G

VIOLET VITALITY

vegan, sweet

Packed with rich phytochemicals that contribute to the health and well-being of all of the body's cells and systems, the superfoods in this smoothie unleash plentiful nutrients including B vitamins, vitamin C, antioxidants, anti-inflammatory agents, and fiber. The concoction also contains unique enzymes and oils that support optimal health by supplying the essentials and protecting against illness and disease.

18 OUNCES

1 cup blackberries
½ cup pineapple
¼" piece ginger, peeled
1 cup green tea, cooled

1. In the 18-ounce NutriBullet cup, combine all ingredients.
2. Blend until all ingredients are thoroughly liquefied and combined, 30–60 seconds.
3. Consume immediately, or store with an airtight lid in the refrigerator for no more than 3–4 hours.

PER SERVING

CALORIES: 103	FAT: 1 G	PROTEIN: 2 G
SODIUM: 2 MG	FIBER: 9 G	
CARBOHYDRATES: 25 G		SUGAR: 15 G

APPENDIX: SMOOTHIES BY TYPE

Vegan

All-Healing Aloe
Antioxidant Alleviator
Antioxidants Galore!
Apple and Spice
Apple Pie
Away with Arthritis!
Awesome Aloe Vera
Awesome Avocado
Awesome Oxidative Reversal
Ayurveda Cure-All
Bananas for Bananas!
Beet the Bloat
Belly Blend
Berries for Better Bellies
Berry-Banana Bloat-Buster
Berry Beet Treat
Berry, Berry Melony
Berry Breathe-Easy
Better Breast Health
Blasting Berries
Blue Juice
Brain-Boosting "Chocolate" Milk for Two!
Brains, Beauty, and Brawn
Broccoli Blend
Calming Cabbage Cooler
Cantaloupe Cure
Carrot-Broccoli Blast-Off
Cashew Milk
Clean Bean Antioxidant Blend
Cleansing Cucumber Carrot
Clear Complexion Cocktail
Cognitive Creation
Constipation Cure
Cool Blue Cantaloupe Cleanse
Cs for Cognition
Cucumber Cooler
Cucumbers for Cooler Complexion
Culinary Creations for "Cuts"
Dark Defender
Delicious Defense
Delicious Detox
Eden Elixir
Energetic Greens
Energizing Elixir
Fatigue Zapper
Fend Off Inflammatory Disease
Ferocious Five-Pound Fighter
Fiberful Fantasia
Fighting Figs
Filling Fiber
Fit and Fiberful
Flu Fighter
Funny Tummy Fixer
Garlicky Greens
Ginger Up
Go Green!
Grapes for Great Health
Grapes for Greatness
Great Garlic!
Great Grape Recovery
Great Green Gracefulness
Great "Green" Green Tea
Great Green Tomato
Green Grace
Green Greatness
Green Your Digestion
Greens for Great Hearts
Greens for Greater Thinking
Hangover Healer
Healthy Beets for Regular Beats
Heart Health Helper
Honeydew for Happy Thoughts
Hydrating Honeydew
Immunity Booster
Keep It Clean!
Kiwi Clarity
Kiwi-Kale Creation
Kiwi-Melon for Maintenance
Kiwi-Peach for Better Beats
Kiwis for Creativity
Mango-Melon Mender
Maximum Results
Melons Mend All!
Men's Mental Mender
Merry Melons
Metabolism Maximizer
Mighty Melon-Citrus
Morning Sickness Mender
Muscle-Maintaining Nut-Milk
Muscle Motivator
Nuts about Heart Health
Nuts about Protein
Nutty for Blood Health
Oh, Mama! Omegas!
Omega Fix with Flax Seed
Peach Cobbler
Perfect Peachy Protein
Pomegranate for Prevention
Potent Pineapple Protection
Powerful Popeye Potion
Prickly Pear
Prickly Pear for Perfection
Prunes for Prevention
Purple Peaches for Prevention
Purple Purifying Pineapple
Rapid Raspberry Rev-Up
Respiratory Relief
Rich Reversal
Savory Skin Saver
Simple Savory Smoothie
Skinny Sensation
Sparkling Strawberry
Spice Is Nice!
Spicy Blue Blend
Spicy Pear Purifier
Spicy Sickness Soother
Spicy Sweetness
Sweet and Spicy Greens
Sweet Celery Celebration
Sweet Citrus Cincher
Sweet Citrus-Pear
Sweet Citrus Spin
Sweet Dreams
Sweet Green Apple-Pear
Sweet Green Skin Machine
Sweet Sexual Health
Sweet Soothing Citrus
Sweet, Spicy Simplicity
Sweet Spinach
Sweet Splendid Greens
Tempting Tomato Twist
Tropical Temptation
Tropical Top-Notch Twist
Tropical Tummy Treat
Vanilla Almond Milk to Benefit All!
Veggies for Vision
Veggies for Vitality
Very Veggie
Violet Vitality
Vitamin "C"ancer Prevention
Walnut Wonder
Weight-Loss Success
Wonders of Watermelon
Yummy Menopause Mixer

Green

All-Healing Aloe
Apple Pie
Awesome Aloe Vera
Awesome Oxidative Reversal
Ayurveda Cure-All
Beet the Bloat
Berries for Better Bellies
Better Breast Health
Cantaloupe Cure
Clean Bean Antioxidant Blend
Cognitive Creation
Constipation Cure
Cool Blue Cantaloupe Cleanse
Cucumber Cooler
Dark Defender

Delicious Defense
Energetic Greens
Fend Off Inflammatory Disease
Ferocious Five-Pound Fighter
Fiberful Fantasia
Filling Fiber
Fit and Fiberful
Flu Fighter
Funny Tummy Fixer
Garlicky Greens
Go Green!
Grapes for Greatness
Great Garlic!
Great Green Gracefulness
Great "Green" Green Tea
Great Green Tomato
Green Grace
Green Greatness
Greens for Great Hearts
Greens for Greater Thinking
Green Your Digestion
Healthy Beets for Regular Beats
Immunity Booster
Kiwi Clarity
Kiwi-Kale Creation
Kiwi-Peach for Better Beats
Maximum Results
Men's Mental Mender
Metabolism Maximizer
Muscle Motivator
Nuts about Heart Health
Pomegranate for Prevention
Powerful Popeye Potion
Prickly Pear
Prunes for Prevention
Savory Skin Saver
Skinny Sensation
Spicy Pear Purifier
Sweet and Spicy Greens
Sweet Citrus-Pear
Sweet Citrus Spin
Sweet Green Apple-Pear
Sweet Green Skin Machine
Sweet, Spicy Simplicity
Sweet Spinach
Sweet Splendid Greens
Veggies for Vision
Veggies for Vitality
Very Veggie
Vitamin "C"ancer Prevention
Weight-Loss Success
Wonders of Watermelon

Sweet

A, B, Cs
Aches, Be Gone!
Acne Alleviator
All-Healing Aloe
Amazing Aminos
Antioxidant Alleviator
Antioxidants Galore!
Apple and Spice
Apple Pie
Away with Arthritis!
Awesome Aloe Vera
Awesome Avocado
Awesome Oxidative Reversal
Ayurveda Cure-All
Bananas for Bananas!
Bananas for Better Blood Sugar
Beet the Bloat
Belly Blend
Berries for Better Bellies
Berries Full of Bs
Berry-Banana Blend
Berry-Banana Bloat-Buster
Berry Beet Treat
Berry, Berry Melony
Berry Blasts for Muscle Mass
Berry Blend for Bone Health
Berry Breathe-Easy
Berry, Merry Skin
Better Breast Health
Blasting Berries
Blue Juice
Blueberries for Brain Health
Brain-Boosting "Chocolate" Milk for Two!
Brains, Beauty, and Brawn
Cacao Cure for Choco Cravings
Calming Cabbage Cooler
Cancer Combatant
Cantaloupe Cure
Clean Bean Antioxidant Blend
Cleansing Cucumber Carrot
Cognitive Creation
Colitis-Calming Carrot-Citrus-Apple
Constipation Cure
Cool Blue Cantaloupe Cleanse
Cool Colon Cleanser
Creamy, Dreamy Sweetness
Cs for Cognition
Cucumber Cooler
Cucumbers for Cooler Complexion
Culinary Creations for "Cuts"
Dark Defender
Delicious Detox
De-light-fully Delicious!
Eden Elixir
Energetic Greens
Energizing Elixir
Fatigue Fighter
Fatigue Zapper
Fats for Fit Brains
Fend Off Inflammatory Disease
Ferocious Five-Pound Fighter
Fiberful Fantasia
Fighting Figs
Filling Fiber
Fit and Fiberful
Fit Fats for Nerve Functioning
Flexibility Found!
Forgo Inflammation with Fruitiness
Fruits and Flax Seed
Fruity Focus Fixer
Funny Tummy Fixer
Ginger Up
Go Green!
Grapes for Great Health
Grapes for Greatness
Great Grape Recovery
Great Green Gracefulness
Great "Green" Green Tea
Green Grace
Green Greatness
Greens for Great Hearts
Greens for Greater Thinking
Green Your Digestion
Hangover Healer
Healthy Beets for Regular Beats
Honeydew for Happy Thoughts
Hydrating Honeydew
Immunity Booster
Inflammation Immunity
Keep It Clean!
Kiwi Clarity
Kiwi-Kale Creation
Kiwi-Melon for Maintenance
Kiwi-Peach for Better Beats
Kiwis for Creativity
Mangoes for Moodiness
Mango-Melon Mender
Maximum Results
Melons Mend All!
Merry Melons
Metabolism Maximizer
Mighty Melon-Citrus
Minty Raspberry Reversal
Mood Maximizer
Morning Sickness Mender
Muscle-Maintaining Nut-Milk
Muscle Maximizer
Muscle Motivator
Nuts about Heart Health
Nuts about Protein
Nutty for Blood Health
Oh, Mama! Omegas!
Omega Fix with Flax Seed
Omegas for Optimal Brain Functioning
Omegas Unleashed
Orange Protection and Prevention
Peach Cobbler

Peachy Perfection
Peachy Protection
Perfect Papaya Prevention
Perfect Peachy Protein
Pomegranate for Prevention
Pomegranate for Prostate
Potent Pineapple Protection
Powerful Popeye Potion
Powerhouse-a-Plenty
Pregnancy Perfection
Prepare with Pears!
Prickly Pear
Prickly Pear for Perfection
Protein-Packed Perfection
Prunes for Prevention
Purple Peaches for Prevention
Purple Purifying Pineapple
Quick Carrot Cleanse
Rapid Raspberry Rev-Up
Raspberries for Recovery
Respiratory Refresher
Respiratory Relief
Rich Regulator
Rich Reversal
Skinny Sensation
Sore Throat Soother
Sparkling Strawberry
Spice Is Nice!
Spicy Blue Blend
Spicy Pear Purifier
Spicy Sweetness
Strawberries for Stamina
Sun-Damage Soother
Sweet and Simple Cell Protection
Sweet and Spicy Greens
Sweet Celery Celebration
Sweet Citrus Cincher
Sweet Citrus-Pear
Sweet Citrus Spin
Sweet Dreams
Sweet Green Apple-Pear
Sweet Green Skin Machine
Sweet Peach Prevention
Sweet PMS Savior
Sweet Potato Protein Perfection
Sweet Sexual Health
Sweet Soothing Citrus
Sweet, Spicy Simplicity
Sweet Spinach
Sweet Splendid Greens
The Perfect Protein Prescription
Tropical Inflammation Tamer
Tropical Temptation
Tropical Top-Notch Twist
Tropical Tummy Treat
Tropical Yummy Yogurt
Veggies for Vision
Very Cherry Yogurt Parfait
Violet Vitality
Vitamin "C"ancer Prevention
Vitamin C for Supple Skin
Walnut Wonder
Weight-Loss Success
Wonders of Watermelon
Youthful Yogurt Bliss
Yummy Menopause Mixer
Yummy Yazzberry Yogurt

Savory

Broccoli Blend
Carrot-Broccoli Blast-Off
Clear Complexion Cocktail
Delicious Defense
Flu Fighter
Garlicky Greens
Great Garlic!
Great Green Tomato
Heart Health Helper
Men's Mental Mender
Savory Skin Saver
Simple Savory Smoothie
Spicy Sickness Soother
Tempting Tomato Twist
Veggies for Vitality
Very Veggie

Paleo

A, B, Cs
All-Healing Aloe
Antioxidants Galore!
Apple and Spice
Apple Pie
Awesome Aloe Vera
Awesome Avocado
Awesome Oxidative Reversal
Ayurveda Cure-All
Bananas for Bananas!
Bananas for Better Blood Sugar
Beet the Bloat
Belly Blend
Berries for Better Bellies
Berry Beet Treat
Berry, Berry Melony
Blue Juice
Brain-Boosting "Chocolate" Milk for Two!
Brains, Beauty, and Brawn
Cacao Cure for Choco Cravings
Calming Cabbage Cooler
Cashew Milk
Clean Bean Antioxidant Blend
Cleansing Cucumber Carrot
Clear Complexion Cocktail
Cognitive Creation
Colitis-Calming Carrot-Citrus-Apple
Constipation Cure
Cucumber Cooler
Delicious Defense
Fighting Figs
Funny Tummy Fixer
Garlicky Greens
Great Garlic!
Great Grape Recovery
Great Green Gracefulness
Green Greatness
Green Your Digestion
Greens for Great Hearts
Hangover Healer
Healthy Beets for Regular Beats
Honeydew for Happy Thoughts
Kiwi-Peach for Better Beats
Melons Mend All
Merry Melons
Minty Raspberry Reversal
Muscle-Maintaining Nut-Milk
Muscle Motivator
Nuts about Heart Health
Nuts about Protein
Nutty for Blood Health
Oh, Mama! Omegas!
Omega Fix with Flax Seed
Peachy Perfection
Perfect Peachy Protein
Potent Pineapple Protection
Prickly Pear
Savory Skin Saver
Sore Throat Soother
Spice Is Nice!
Spicy Blue Blend
Spicy Sickness Soother
Sweet and Simple Cell Protection
Sweet and Spicy Greens
Sweet Citrus-Pear
Sweet Citrus Spin
Sweet Green Skin Machine
Sweet Peach Prevention
Sweet Sexual Health
Sweet Soothing Citrus
Sweet Spinach
Tempting Tomato Twist
Tropical Temptation
Tropical Top-Notch Twist
Tropical Tummy Treat
Vanilla Almond Milk to Benefit All!
Very Veggie

INDEX

ABOUT THE AUTHOR

Britt Brandon lives in Jensen Beach, FL with her husband and three children. She has received her certifications as a Fitness Nutrition Specialist and Personal Trainer from the International Sports Sciences Association, and is currently pursuing a Master's of Science degree in Exercise Science and Health Promotion at Florida Atlantic University. She has written eleven books for Adams Media on topics including clean eating, prenatal health and nutrition, and healing ingredients such as apple cider vinegar, coconut oil, aloe vera, and ginger. She can be contacted at her blog, *www.UltimateFitMom.com*, or via e-mail at *brittabrandon@yahoo.com*.